SLAUGHTERHOUSE-FIVE

NOTES

including
- *Life and Background*
- *Introduction to the Novel*
- *A Historical Introduction to the Bombing of Dresden*
- *A Brief Synopsis*
- *List of Characters*
- *Chronology of the Events in* Slaughterhouse-Five
- *Critical Commentaries*
- *Battleground Map of* Slaughterhouse-Five
- *Critical Essays*
    Predestination and Free Will in *Slaughterhouse-Five*
    The Anti-Hero and Billy Pilgrim
    The Vonnegut Humor
    The Presence of the Narrator in *Slaughterhouse-Five*
    The Song of Roland and *Slaughterhouse-Five*
    Slaughterhouse-Five on Film
- *Review Questions and Essay Topics*
- *Vonnegut's Published Works*
- *Selected Bibliography*

by
Dennis Stanton Smith, M.A.
University of Colorado, Boulder

Wiley Publishing, Inc.

Editor
Dennis Stanton Smith, M.A., University of Colorado

Consulting Editor
James L. Roberts, Ph.D., Department of English, University of Nebraska

Composition
Wiley Indianapolis Composition Services

CliffsNotes™ *Slaughterhouse-Five*

Published by:
Wiley Publishing, Inc.
111 River Street
Hoboken, NJ 07030
www.wiley.com

Copyright © 1997 Wiley Publishing, Inc., Hoboken, NJ
ISBN: 978-0-8220-1205-4
Printed in the United States of America
15 14 13 12 11
1O/TQ/RR/QU/IN
Published by Wiley Publishing, Inc., Hoboken, NJ
Published simultaneously in Canada

CONTENTS

Center Spread: Battleground Map of *Slaughterhouse-Five*

SLAUGHTERHOUSE-FIVE

Notes

LIFE AND BACKGROUND

Some of Kurt Vonnegut's critics have called him a skeptic, a pessimist, a fatalist, a malcontent—everything from a cynic to a worrywart—for his seemingly depressive view of civilization. Others have more accurately described him as a cultural scientist, a prophetic environmentalist offering humankind a glimmer of hope. Throughout much of Vonnegut's writing, one theme resounds again and again: Like the toll of a funeral bell, he warns civilization that time on Earth is running out. In a number of his lectures and autobiographical works, he counsels that one day soon, we will all go "belly-up like guppies in a neglected fishbowl." Suggesting an epitaph for our planet, he offers, "We could have saved it, but we were too darn cheap and lazy."

One of the things that shapes Vonnegut's perception of civilization is the academic training he received while earning a master's degree in anthropology from the University of Chicago. He contends that because anthropology teaches students to seek explanations for humans' comfort and discomfort in culture, society, and history, his villains are never mere individuals: Instead, they are the culture, the society, and the history studied by anthropologists. In *Hocus Pocus*, for example, he says that the primary character, excluding himself, is imperialism.

The son and grandson of architects, Kurt Vonnegut, Jr., was born on November 11, 1922, in Indianapolis, Indiana. The Vonneguts, a family of German descent, held beliefs of pacifism and atheism—beliefs that figure prominently in Vonnegut's works. Educated in Indianapolis, his journalistic endeavors began as a reporter for his high-school newspaper and continued after he entered Cornell University in 1940 as a chemistry major, writing for the student newspaper.

The bombing of Pearl Harbor in December 1941 changed Vonnegut's life. Despite his feelings of pacifism, he volunteered for military service. He was trained to operate a 240-millimeter howitzer, but because he had some university academic credit, and because he had been in the Reserve Officers Training Corps, the army sent him back to college at Carnegie Tech as part of the Army Specialized Training Program. When the army needed manpower for the invasion of Europe, he was sent to the infantry. In the 106th Infantry Division, assigned to defend a seventy-five mile stretch of the Luxembourg-Germany border, he was made a battalion intelligence scout, requiring him to sneak out ahead of Allied lines and observe the enemy.

In the winter of 1944, the Germans began their last, major military offensive of the war: the Battle of the Bulge. Vonnegut's unit was unprepared for combat and was quickly overrun by the German army. Vonnegut was captured and placed in a work camp in Dresden, Germany. Along with ninety-nine other American prisoners, he worked in a factory making a vitamin-enriched malt syrup for pregnant women.

The bombing of Dresden, lasting from February 13, 1945, to April 17, 1945, destroyed much of the city—hospitals, schools, churches, nursing homes, and apartment buildings. Up to 135,000 inhabitants were killed. After the air raid, Vonnegut was put on detail to remove and cremate the corpses that rotted throughout the city. Thousands of human carcasses were incinerated on huge funeral pyres or with flame throwers. Vonnegut's perception of this horrific misery was amplified further during the days of his liberation. Confined in the Russian zone, he spent time with Nazi concentration camp survivors from Eastern Europe—particularly, from Auschwitz and from Birkenau—listening to these survivors' gruesome stories of the Holocaust.

After the war, he returned to Indianapolis and married his childhood sweetheart, Jane Cox, whom he had met in kindergarten. He entered the University of Chicago as a graduate student in anthropology, and in 1947, he accepted a public relations job with General Electric. Three years later, he quit his job to devote full time to writing. In 1952, he published his first novel, *Player Piano*, a work based somewhat on his experiences in the corporate environment.

Player Piano, like Vonnegut's next two novels, *The Sirens of Titan* (1959) and *Mother Night* (1961), met with little success. His fourth novel, *Cat's Cradle* (1963), became a cult favorite of the counter culture, and he acquired an underground reputation; the novel was especially revered on college campuses in the sixties. Vonnegut followed this work with an assortment of reviews, essays, and speeches compiled in *Wampeters, Foma & Granfalloons* (1965), and then returned to writing fiction with *Slaughterhouse-Five*. Published in 1969, during the war in Vietnam, it received critical acclaim and became a bestseller. Vonnegut's use of the massive, unrelenting Allied firebombing of Dresden in World War II as the pivotal image of the novel was a natural analogy to the United States' bombing of North Vietnam "back to the Stone Age."

Having made his reputation as a novelist, Vonnegut turned to the theater in 1970, with *Happy Birthday, Wanda June*, a revised version of a play he had written years before under the title *Penelope*. The play ran for 142 performances off-Broadway and was moderately successful with critics. In 1972, he wrote a play for the National Television Network, *Between Time and Timbuktu, or Prometheus-5*. This endeavor was not so much a new work as a series of scenes from his novels and plays, strung together with a connecting plot. Also, *Welcome to the Monkey House*, a collection of his short stories that included some published earlier in *Canary in a Cathouse*, was issued in 1970.

Vonnegut's next novel—which he claimed would be his last—was published in 1973. *Breakfast of Champions* is a recapitulation of the major themes of Vonnegut's earlier works and is a farewell to his characters, whom he frees in the epilogue. The book met with a great deal of critical and popular acclaim. In 1976, he published *Slapstick*, which opens with his confession that the book will be his closest attempt yet at autobiography. Couched as a fictional story about Dr. Wilbur Daffodil-11 Swain, the final president of the United States, and his twin sister, Eliza, the novel is a tribute to Vonnegut's sister, Alice Vonnegut, who died of cancer at forty-one.

Most readers were probably not surprised when Kilgore Trout reappeared in Vonnegut's next work of fiction, *Jailbird* (1979). The novel begins with this admission: "Yes—Kilgore Trout is back again.

He could not make it on the outside. That is no disgrace. A lot of good people can't make it on the outside." We get the feeling that Vonnegut is speaking more about himself than about Kilgore Trout. Like much of his work, *Jailbird* is a social commentary. In it, Walter F. Starbuck, a former official in President Richard M. Nixon's administration, is released from prison following a conviction in the Watergate conspiracy. Events following Starbuck's release culminate in his being hired by a titanic corporation that effectively controls over one-quarter of the U.S. economy. Vonnegut uses Starbuck's being hired by this industrial giant to point out the corruptness of U.S. industry, how there is no rhyme or reason for the decisions that are made daily by huge corporations. People become slaves to technology, and industry's main concern is increasing profit at workers' expense.

Vonnegut followed up *Jailbird* with *Palm Sunday* (1981), which he subtitled *An Autobiographical Collage*. In this work, he plays with different forms of writing, mixing together such different genres as speeches, letters, articles, and even a musical comedy. Always willing to push the limits of traditional forms of writing, *Palm Sunday* is one of Vonnegut's boldest attempts at experimental writing.

Over the next six years, Vonnegut published three novels, all of which deal with a son's relationship with his father, a relationship that is usually dysfunctional. In *Deadeye Dick* (1982), Rudy Waltz recounts growing up in Midland City, Ohio, with a father who is more interested in gun collecting than in having a meaningful relationship with his family. The title of the novel comes from people nicknaming Rudy "Deadeye Dick" after he accidentally shoots and kills a pregnant woman while playing with one of his father's guns.

Galapagos (1985), Vonnegut's next novel, is narrated by Leon Trout, Kilgore Trout's son, who is as bitter about life as his father was. Vonnegut addresses the problems of human greed and damaging technological advancements. The setting for the book is the islands of Galapagos, where Charles Darwin studied the animal life and then wrote *Origin of Species*, outlining his theory of evolution. Leon Trout's ghost, which has survived from the year 1986 to the year one million A.D., recounts the many mistakes humans have made in bringing about our planet's demise.

In *Bluebeard* (1987), Vonnegut's main character, Rabo Karabekian, has a bad family life, but he is able to overcome the alienation felt by so many of Vonnegut's characters. As an artist, he immerses himself in his art and in the paintings of great modern artists. He discovers that there is a world inside himself that is nurturing and nondestructive. Through his art, Rabo recreates his life and affirms his self-worth.

Since 1990, Vonnegut has published two major works, *Hocus Pocus* (1990) and *Fates Worse Than Death: An Autobiographical Collage of the 1980s* (1991). *Hocus Pocus* is a fictional work concerning Eugene Debs Hartke, who is fired from Tarkington College in New York and then hired by the New York State Maximum Security Adult Correctional Institution, which is directly across a lake from the college. When the prisoners at the correctional facility escape, they hold hostages at the college, and Hartke is eventually made warden at the college, renamed the Tarkington State Reformatory.

Fates Worse Than Death is similar to *Palm Sunday* in that it contains various speeches, essays, and autobiographical commentary addressing Vonnegut's opinions on a broad range of issues. Vonnegut characterizes the work as "a sequel, not that anyone has clamored for one, to a book called *Palm Sunday*."

Known for his self-deprecating style, Vonnegut continues to ridicule his own work while at the same time staking out a claim as one of the preeminent American writers since World War II. In a 1996 interview, in which he promoted the cinematic release of *Mother Night*, he claimed that his best work had been published prior to his reaching the age of fifty-five. Commenting on his increased popularity in the late 1990s, he said, "My life is essentially a garage sale now."

INTRODUCTION TO THE NOVEL

Slaughterhouse-Five is a work of literary fiction that combines historical, sociological, psychological, science-fiction, and biographical elements. Unlike novels based on traditional forms, Vonnegut's novel does not fit a model that stresses plot, character conflict, and climax. There is no protagonist/antagonist conflict, nor is the novel structured by the usual sequence of boy-meets-girl, boy-loses-girl, boy-gets-girl. With *Slaughterhouse-Five*, the novel's traditional form is dislodged, and Vonnegut offers us a multifaceted, many-dimensional view of fantasy and rock-hard reality.

Disruption of the novel's traditional form is not unique with *Slaughterhouse-Five*. Vonnegut's form is similar to the works of other authors writing after World War II, including Joseph Heller and John Barth. For Vonnegut, *Slaughterhouse-Five*'s form grew out of events arising from his World War II experiences, particularly the horrors of the months-long Dresden air raids. Because he views the Dresden bombing as senseless, everything Vonnegut writes describing the bombing has to feel senseless as well.

Vonnegut was evolving as a novelist just when academicians were pronouncing what they termed "the death of the novel." Critics argued that modern life, with its political assassinations, the threat of nuclear war, and the dilemma of the war in Vietnam, made it impossible for a novelist to offer any logical assessment of reality. For instance, the events in *Slaughterhouse-Five* are not told chronologically; an episode in the present triggers an episode in the past or into the future. Even its title page is radically different from other novels' title pages: To its supplemental label, *The Children's Crusade,* *Slaughterhouse-Five* adds a second subtitle: *A Duty-Dance with Death.* In addition, Vonnegut includes a "telegraphic schizophrenic" narrative explaining who he is and where he has been. We are engaged in the Dresden story even before the novel begins: Not until Chapter Two does the actual narrative of Billy Pilgrim's odyssey start.

A HISTORICAL INTRODUCTION TO THE BOMBING OF DRESDEN

The bombing of Dresden began February 13, 1945, and lasted through April 17—a period of two months—yet even today, it remains one of the most controversial military decisions in modern warfare. Why this premier cultural city was devastated during World War II continues to be clouded in mystery. Two contradictory reasons for the bombing have emerged. First, with the Russian army advancing on the Eastern Front, German forces were being solidified to repel the Russians and needed to be "softened," thereby allowing the Russians to advance more easily. Second, with the war winding down and the Western Allies and Russians realizing that conquered land would be up for grabs, the bombing would demonstrate to the Russians the immense power of the Western Allies (the United States, Great Britain, and France) and would deter the Russians from grabbing land; besides, if the Russians occupied land that the Western Allies wanted, the bombing would devastate the land, making it worthless.

Code-named Thunderclap, a plan put forth by Allied military leaders to bomb sequentially one large German city after another, the Dresden destruction began the night of February 13, 1945, when Britain's Royal Air Force sent planes to bomb the city. In all, the Royal Air Force sent 800 aircraft over Dresden, dropping incendiary bombs that caused massive devastation—not because of their initial impact, but because of the fires that ensued. The following afternoon, the U.S. 8th Air Force assaulted Dresden with 400 bombers, then continued with 200 more planes on February 15. A brief respite ensued after these February bombings, but on March 2, the U.S. 8th Air Force again bombed the city, using 400 more aircraft. Finally, the destruction of Dresden concluded with the 8th Air Force sending 572 bombers over the city on April 17.

The number of persons killed during the two-month bombing of Dresden is impossible to pinpoint precisely. Estimated casualties range from 35,000 up to 135,000, a disparity due in part to the chaotic nature of all wartime bombings. The details of this tragedy are complicated by the great number of refugees flooding into Dresden from the outlying regions, desperately hoping to escape the oncoming Russian army.

Information about the bombing remained secret until 1978, when the U.S. Air Force declassified many of the documents concerning Thunderclap. However, the true reasons for the exorbitant bombing remain ambiguous. The Allies insist that Dresden housed military installations such as barracks, camps comprised of makeshift huts, and at least one munitions storage depot. However, the hutted camps were full of refugees, not soldiers, and the munitions storage depot housed munitions stores used in mining. In addition, the Allies claim that Dresden was the site of a communications center that needed to be destroyed in order to help the Russian Allies approaching from the east. Clearly, many citizens in both Britain and the United States were so outraged by the Germans' bombing of London earlier in the war that they were happy to see a substantial retaliation of some sort. There was little mourning for Dresden by the Allies.

Given the military reasons advanced for bombing Dresden, the issue is even more clouded when we consider the political reasons behind the action. A Royal Air Force memo cites the need to strike the German army behind its front line, but continues with the belief that the bombing will also show the advancing Russians the power of the Western Allied forces. As World War II wound down, some Russian and Western Allied leaders openly described the final war campaigns as a victors' "land-grab" operation. However, after the war, a leading Russian general suggested that the Allies destroyed cities in eastern Germany bound to fall under Russian control with the sole purpose of leaving worthless rubble to them.

Whatever the reason—or reasons—for the Allies' bombing of Dresden, the fact remains clear that the city was destroyed and civilians were killed to a greater extent by far than ever occurred in the Germans' bombing of London. The image of a destroyed Dresden that once housed one of the greatest art collections in the world and was truly one of the renowned musical and architectural centers can still cause entirely different reactions, ranging from those who say that the bombing was necessary for military and political reasons, to those who claim that the bombing was a senseless and unnecessary act, aimed only at destroying German neighborhoods where strategic installations did not even exist.

A BRIEF SYNOPSIS

Slaughterhouse-Five is an account of Billy Pilgrim's capture and incarceration by the Germans during the last years of World War II, and scattered throughout the narrative are episodes from Billy's life both before and after the war, and from his travels to the planet Tralfamadore (Trawl-**fahm**-uh-door). Billy is able to move both forwards and backwards through his lifetime in an arbitrary cycle of events. Enduring the tedious life of a 1950s optometrist in Ilium, New York, he is the lover of a former pornographic movie star on the planet Tralfamadore and simultaneously an American prisoner of war (POW) in Nazi Germany.

Vonnegut uses Billy's ability to travel in time as a device to evoke a wide range of scenes from Billy's life. The multidimensional panorama points out the importance of cyclical time and psychological experience during events that receive equal emphasis in linear time. While some scenes become so jumbled that they seem to have no cause or effect, we must remember Vonnegut's comments on the title page. He suggests that this narrative is "schizophrenic," and he invites us to become psychologists helping Billy make sense of his life.

Slaughterhouse-Five's central topic is the horror of the Dresden bombing. As a witness to the destruction, Billy confronts fundamental questions about the meanings of life and death. Traumatized by the events in Dresden, Billy can provide no answers. As a soldier, he is dislocated in a system where there is no reward, no punishment, and no justice. Although his life as an optometrist, a husband, and a father is materially fulfilling, he is unable to find peace of mind because of the trauma he suffered in Dresden.

Ultimately, Billy reconciles this trauma with the acceptance of the Tralfamadorian doctrine that there is no such thing as free will: Billy cannot change the past, the present, or the future. In the final analysis, Vonnegut suggests that life is like a simple, meaningless limerick, a nonsensical verse that never ends because it continuously repeats itself. At the beginning of *Slaughterhouse-Five*, the bird's song asks, "*Poo-tee-weet?*"; at the end of the novel, Billy hears the bird still asking the same simple, meaningless question.

LIST OF CHARACTERS

Billy Pilgrim

The central character of *Slaughterhouse-Five*. A pacifist, a soldier, a prisoner of war, and an optometrist (someone who prescribes corrective lenses for people who have visual defects), Billy is the epitome of a mild-mannered Everyman who adapts to life's situations rather than challenge them. He feels it is better to turn the other cheek than to suffer the guilt of being offensive—the only "aggressive" action Billy takes during the novel is his committing himself into a mental ward. He becomes "unstuck in time" and travels to other times and places.

Bernard V. O'Hare

A former soldier and the narrator's comrade from the Nazis' POW camps in the 1940s. Some twenty years after the war has ended, O'Hare accompanies the narrator on a visit back to Dresden.

Gerhard Müller

A taxi driver in post-World War II Dresden, he befriends the narrator and Bernard V. O'Hare when they return to that city in 1967.

Mary O'Hare

The wife of Bernard V. O'Hare, she rebukes the narrator concerning the novel he intends to write, contending that he will make war attractive by imposing heroic, adult maturity on the immature boy-soldier participants.

Roland Weary

A bully and a braggart, he is a foil to Billy Pilgrim, illustrating the contrast between his aggressive degeneracy and Billy's pacifism.

The Scouts

Two unnamed American soldiers, their job is to slip behind enemy lines and gather essential information about the enemy.

Edgar Derby

A fellow POW at the Dresden camp. Elected leader by the other American prisoners, he is executed one month after the Dresden bombing for stealing a teapot.

Paul Lazzaro

A former car thief from Cicero, Illinois, he promises a dying Roland Weary that he will have Billy Pilgrim killed. Lazzaro's promise is carried out in 1976.

Mr. Pilgrim

Billy's smug, self-righteous, and patriarchal father; when Billy is a child, his father throws him into the deep end of a pool to teach him how to swim, and to shock him into assertive behavior. Mr. Pilgrim is accidentally shot and killed in a hunting accident while Billy is on military maneuvers in South Carolina.

Mrs. Pilgrim

Billy's mother, a self-sacrificing martyr but spiritually empty; eventually, Billy places her in a nursing home.

Valencia Merble Pilgrim

Billy's wife and Lionel Merble's daughter, she is a puppet in her father's business dealings and Billy's material success; Valencia dies from carbon-monoxide poisoning after an automobile accident.

Lionel Merble

Billy's father-in-law and a member of the John Birch Society; he owns the Ilium School of Optometry, from which Billy graduates.

Barbara Pilgrim

The daughter of Billy and Valencia and the personification of middle-class hypocrisy and indifference. She has little concern for her father's condition, but she worries greatly about what people will think—how it will reflect on her.

Robert Pilgrim

The son of Billy and Valencia, he becomes a Green Beret and fights in the Vietnam War.

Eliot Rosewater

Billy's roommate in the veterans' hospital, Eliot is an example of someone who is trying to reinvent himself in order to atone for his wartime atrocities. He introduces Billy to Kilgore Trout's novels.

Kilgore Trout

A science-fiction writer of many novels and an inspiration to Billy, he works as a circulation manager for the *Ilium Gazette*. Absurdly, his books are used as window dressing in a New York City pornography shop.

Harrison Starr

A moviemaker and a critic of the state of the novel in the modern world; he contends that wars happen regardless of what anyone does to prevent them.

Bertram Copeland Rumfoord

A retired brigadier general and the official historian of the U.S. Air Force, he shares a room with Billy in a Vermont hospital after Billy's plane crash.

Lily Rumfoord

The wife of Bertram Copeland Rumfoord.

Lance Rumfoord

A nephew of Bertram Copeland Rumfoord, he is a passenger honeymooning on a yacht that sails by Billy and Valencia's apartment on their wedding night.

Howard W. Campbell, Jr.

An American turned traitor, he writes propaganda for the Nazis. He functions as a characterization of supremacist chauvinism carried to extreme absurdity.

The English Colonel

The leader of the English officers at the POW camp where Billy is initially taken after being captured.

Werner Gluck

A tall, weak, sixteen-year-old German guard at the Dresden POW camp.

The Maori

A brown-skinned aborigine from New Zealand; also a POW, he is teamed with Billy to remove corpses from Dresden's rubble.

The Narrator/Kurt Vonnegut

A part-time character strongly represented in *Slaughterhouse-Five*. As the narrator, Vonnegut frames his novel with beginning and ending chapters that sketch his own biography, relate how he goes about writing the narrative, and describe how the narrative took on a new form in the process.

Maggie White

A voluptuous dimwit, she is the wife of an optometrist at Billy's wedding anniversary party.

Wild Bob

An American infantry colonel who loses his entire regiment in battle.

Montana Wildhack

A movie star and sex symbol featured in pornographic magazines, she is Billy's mate in the Tralfamadore zoo.

Marine Corps Major

The speaker at a Lions Club luncheon who tells Billy that he should be proud of his son, Robert, fighting in Vietnam.

CHRONOLOGY OF THE EVENTS IN *SLAUGHTERHOUSE-FIVE*

1922 Billy Pilgrim is born in Ilium, New York (Chapter Two).

1934 Billy and his family vacation at the Grand Canyon and Carlsbad Caverns (Chapter Five).

1944 Assigned as a chaplain's assistant, Billy is on military maneuvers in South Carolina when his father dies after being accidentally shot by a friend while hunting (Chapter Two).
December Billy joins an infantry regiment fighting in Luxembourg. After the regiment is decimated by the German army during the Battle of the Bulge, he and three others, including Roland Weary, find themselves behind German lines. Billy and Weary are captured after three days of wandering (Chapter Two).
December 23 After being forcibly marched into Germany, Billy and the other American prisoners are loaded into boxcars bound for eastern Germany (Chapter Three).
December 25 The trainload of American prisoners begins

to creep eastward after sitting idle for two days (Chapter Three).

1945   **January 3** Roland Weary dies of gangrene (Chapter Four).
January 4 After ten days of traveling, Billy's train stops at a prison camp originally built as an annihilation camp for Russian POWs. Billy and his fellow prisoners are forced from the train, after which they are deloused and given overcoats (Chapter Four).
January 5 They are shipped by train to a prison camp in Dresden, Germany, where they are housed in building five, previously used as a slaughterhouse (Chapter Six).
February 13–April 17 Dresden is destroyed by American and British bombers; according to some historians, 135,000 people, including civilians and military personnel, are killed (Chapter Eight).
The army honorably discharges Billy (Chapter Two).

1948   **Spring** During his final year at the Ilium School of Optometry, Billy voluntarily commits himself into a veterans' hospital ward for nonviolent mental patients. In the hospital, he meets Eliot Rosewater, who introduces him to Kilgore Trout's science-fiction novels (Chapter Five).
Billy graduates from the Ilium School of Optometry and marries Valencia Merble (Chapter Five).

1957   **Autumn** Billy is elected president of the Ilium, New York, Lions Club (Chapter Two).

1964   The narrator visits Bernard V. O'Hare, an old war buddy, to discuss the bombing of Dresden (Chapter One).
1964–1966 During these two years, the narrator teaches creative writing at the University of Iowa (Chapter One), and Billy meets Kilgore Trout, the science-fiction writer whom Eliot Rosewater talked about, for the first time (Chapter Eight).

1965   Billy commits his mother into a nursing home (Chapter Two).

1967   The narrator and Bernard V. O'Hare return to Dresden to recount their wartime experiences (Chapters One and Ten).
August Now a past president of the Lions Club, Billy attends a Club luncheon, where a Marine Corps major com-

ments that he should by proud of his son, Robert, a Green Beret fighting in Vietnam (Chapter Three).

A flying saucer from Tralfamadore kidnaps Billy on his daughter Barbara's wedding night (Chapters Two and Four).

1968 A plane carrying Billy to an optometry convention in Montreal, Canada, crashes on Sugarbush Mountain, Vermont; except for Billy and the copilot, everyone, including Billy's father-in-law, is killed (Chapters Two and Seven).

Valencia, Billy's wife, dies of carbon monoxide poisoning while he is recuperating in a Vermont hospital following the plane crash (Chapter Two).

On the day he returns home from the hospital, Billy goes to New York City, hoping to appear on television to discuss his kidnapping by Tralfamadorians; eventually he appears on a New York City radio talk show (Chapter Nine).

1976 **February 13** As he foresaw, Billy is assassinated in Chicago by a hit man hired by Paul Lazzaro, a fellow soldier during the war; Lazzaro had promised Roland Weary that he would kill Billy to avenge Weary's claim that Billy caused his capture by the Germans after their three days of wandering (Chapter Six).

CRITICAL COMMENTARIES

EPIGRAPH

The four lines of poetry appearing at the beginning of *Slaughterhouse-Five* ("The cattle are lowing . . . ") are used thematically throughout the novel as Billy Pilgrim moves along his pilgrimage. The lyrics of the Christmas carol attest that the newborn baby does not cry. Analogous to the newborn baby is Billy: Throughout most of the wartime sections of *Slaughterhouse-Five*, he does not cry. Only in Chapter Nine, when he is made aware of the suffering horses—perhaps an antithesis to the mooing cattle—does he cry for the first time. Later, as a civilian in Ilium, he cries regularly. And from lyrics in the carol that precede those of the epigraph ("Away in a manger . . . "), Vonnegut leaps across many pages and makes a connection to the American POWs, who spend the night in a stable at an inn outside of Dresden.

CHAPTER ONE

Summary

The narrator begins *Slaughterhouse-Five* by explaining a number of details about the novel, primarily how he came to write it. He maintains, by and large, that the parts about the war are true, although he admits that he has changed people's names. The narrator tells his old war buddy, Bernard V. O'Hare, that he is writing a book about the bombing of Dresden, Germany, and that he would like O'Hare's help. Although O'Hare is doubtful about remembering much about the war, he tells the narrator to come for a visit. Eventually, we are told, the two men revisit Dresden, destroyed by British and American planes in the last days of World War II.

The narrator explains how his aspirations to write a book about the bombing were received negatively by people who asked what he was working on—he is advised that the work is no more than just another inventory of military atrocities. Contacting the air force to obtain information about the Dresden air raids, he discovers that the operation is still classified as top secret: After his experiences in Dresden during the war, he is astonished to think that these events are not common knowledge.

At O'Hare's home, the narrator detects resentment and hostility seething within O'Hare's wife, Mary. Despite her attempts to disrupt their war-story conversation, the two old buddies recall a number of incidents they experienced together. Mary's irritation overwhelms her: She accuses the narrator of planning to write a novel that glorifies war. Giving his word that he will not write such a book—combat cinema heroes like Frank Sinatra and John Wayne will have no part in the tale—the narrator promises that he will call his novel *The Children's Crusade.*

In his bedroom that night, the narrator reads from a book about Dresden's history that O'Hare placed on his bedside table. The book recounts how in 1760, Dresden underwent a siege by the Prussians. He reads of the contrast between the fate of one particular church and the fate of another: The first church was destroyed in flames, while the second survived because the curves of its dome repulsed the Prussian bombs like rain. The book also relates that when young Goethe, a famous German writer, visited Dresden many years after the war, he found the city still greatly in ruin.

While waiting in a motel room for a flight to Frankfurt, Germany, from where he will travel with O'Hare to Dresden, the narrator reads from two books. From *Words for the Wind*, he quotes four lines of a Theodore Roethke poem that question the reality of wakefulness and make a statement about forging ahead as duty dictates. Next he refers to a work by Erika Ostrovsky about a French writer who was a soldier in World War I. Finally Vonnegut turns to a copy of the Bible. He quotes from the Old Testament story of Sodom and Gomorrah. Conceding that the people in both cities were contemptible, and that the world was better off without them, he empathizes with Lot's wife, who, failing to heed God's edict and glancing back on the destruction, was turned into a pillar of salt. He identifies with her because her last deed was so *human*. He concludes the first chapter by apologizing that his "war book," *Slaughterhouse-Five*, is a failure because it was written by a pillar of salt.

Commentary

The first chapter of *Slaughterhouse-Five* serves more as an introduction or a preamble than as a typical first chapter in a novel. More biographical than fictional, it not only relates a good deal of Kurt Vonnegut's biography, it explains how the novel came to be written.

Chapter One prepares us to understand the characteristics of this nontraditional novel. Vonnegut explains that his early intention was to write in the traditional form of linear plot progression. There would be a beginning, a middle, and an end, and the novel's climax would occur with the destruction of Dresden. However, we soon realize that Vonnegut does not write the novel using this traditional form, perhaps because Billy Pilgrim's life will not be a typical story that we expect.

How Billy will experience time in *Slaughterhouse-Five* is indirectly presented in Chapter One through the use of limericks, nonsensical verses that have no ending. Just as limericks endlessly repeat themselves, so too will Billy's life. Opposed to the cyclical nature of limericks is the flowing water of the Hudson River, which the narrator crosses on his way to Bernard V. O'Hare's house. Vonnegut creates the image of the river as long and narrow, an analogy to demonstrate the nature of chronological time. The narrator's visiting the World's Fair causes him to ponder the nature of time: While the Walt Disney Company's and the Ford Motor Company's exhibitions depict the past, the General Motors' exhibition renders a vision of the future. He again raises the Hudson River analogy, asking himself how wide and deep the present is.

In addition to preparing us for a trip into psychological time, Chapter One introduces the expression *So it goes*: This expression will appear time and time again throughout *Slaughterhouse-Five*. What does the phrase mean? It has been suggested that Vonnegut uses the phrase whenever he chooses to avoid the repetition of brutality. Rather than elaborate the details of a brutal scene or act, he simply elects to say *So it goes*. Also, the phrase is likely a signal calling attention to the concept of predestination. There is no such thing as free will, Vonnegut explains; humankind has no control over its destiny. *So it goes*, he announces. Whatever will be, will be.

The concept of predestination, introduced both by Vonnegut's use of cyclical time and by the expression *So it goes*, furthers our understanding of the meaning behind the two books that the narrator takes with him on his and O'Hare's trip to Dresden. From a book of Theodore Roethke's poems, *Words for the Wind*, Vonnegut quotes from "The Waking":

> I wake to sleep, and take my waking slow.
> I feel my fate in what I cannot fear.
> I learn by going where I have to go.

These lines reinforce the narrator's notion of predetermination. Following the first line's suggestion of a sleep/wakefulness dilemma, the questioning persists. Which is real? Which is illusion? The solution appears in the next two lines. The answer is provided by fate, not free will: The speaker goes, and learns by going where fate's edict directs.

By referring to Ostrovsky's *Céline and His Visions*, Vonnegut makes connections that permeate *Slaughterhouse-Five*. Céline cannot sleep at night because he hears voices in his head, voices that drive him to write bizarre novels. He contends that an artist must suffer to produce art: No art is possible without a dance with death. It is here that the significance of *Slaughterhouse-Five*'s second subtitle, *A Duty-Dance with Death*, is introduced. Billy's pilgrimage is charged with instances of death-dancing. Ever the victim of predestination, Billy's dance, like Céline's, emanates from a noise in his head: the voice of fate.

(Here and in the following chapters, difficult words and phrases are explained.)

- **Guggenheim money**   money from a fund set up in 1925 by Simon Guggenheim and his wife to further the development of scholars and artists by monetarily assisting them in their research endeavors.

- **mustard gas**   An oily liquid used in warfare, it blisters the lungs once it is inhaled.

- **Mutt and Jeff**   comic strip characters introduced in 1904, who were especially popular in the 1940s; Mutt was short and plump, and Jeff was tall and thin.

- **Luftwaffe saber**   the ceremonial sword carried by members of the German air force, known as the Luftwaffe before and during World War II.

- **Hiroshima**   the Japanese city destroyed on August 6, 1945, during World War II, when U.S. forces dropped the first atomic bomb in warfare. Nagasaki, another Japanese city, was destroyed three days later by a second atomic bomb.

- **the Dutch Reformed Church**   a religious organization originating in the Netherlands and known for its belief in predestination.

- *Eheu, fugaces labuntur anni*   Latin, meaning "Alas, the years slip by"; one of the mature observations of the Roman poet Horace (65–8 B.C.).

- **Frank Sinatra**   An American singer and actor born in 1915, he was idolized for his striking good looks and his smooth baritone voice; "ole Blue Eyes" won an Academy Award for his role in *From Here to Eternity*, a war movie.

- **John Wayne**   (1907–79) American actor known for his ruggedness as a self-styled individualist in Western films; he also starred as the hero in numerous World War II films, including *The Sands of Iwo Jima*.

- **Palestine**   often called "the Holy Land"; a historical region between the eastern Mediterranean shore and the Jordan River.

- **Pope Innocent the Third**   pope from 1198 to 1216.

- **Marseilles**   a city in southeast France on an arm of the Mediterranean Sea.

- **Genoa**   a city in northwest Italy on an arm of the Ligurian Sea.

- **Prussians**   citizens of a member-state of republican Germany; Prussia was established in 1918 and formally abolished after World War II.

- *Königstein*   a castle in Dresden in which art treasures were stored during the Allied bombing; also served as a POW camp for important prisoners.

- *Kreuzkirche*   a church in Dresden destroyed during the Allied bombing on February 13, 1945, but since rebuilt.

- *Frauenkirche*   a church in Dresden designed by George Bahr between 1726 and 1743; the church was destroyed during the Allied bombing, but its ruins have been kept as a memorial.

- **Silesia**   a region of central Europe primarily in southwestern Poland and the northern Czech Republic.

- **Goethe**   Johann Wolfgang von Goethe (1749–1832); German writer renowned for his two-part dramatic poem *Faust*, published in 1808 and 1832.

- *Von der Kuppel . . . Das hat der Feind gethan!*   German, meaning "From the cupola of the Church of Our Lady, I saw the sad ruins among the beautiful city buildings; the church sexton praised the architect for having built the bombproof church and cupola. Then the sacristan, musing about the ruins that lay all around us, said critically, using few words: 'The devil has done this!'"

- **Lufthansa**   a German airline company formed in 1926.

- **Theodore Roethke**   An American poet (1908–63), his lyrical verse is characterized by introspection; he was awarded the Pulitzer Prize for his book of poems *The Waking: Poems 1933–1953* (1953).

- **Céline**   Louis-Ferdinand Céline (1894–1961); French writer known for his tortured, angry novels portraying a world without values, beauty, or decency.

- **the Gideon Bible**   the bible used by members of an interdenominational and international society known for placing bibles in hotel rooms.

CHAPTER TWO

Summary

Billy Pilgrim, the main character of this novel-within-a-frame, is introduced through a series of scenes in his life. Included in this series is a summation of the most important events, ranging from his birth through his daughter Barbara's bringing him back home from New York City after he appears on a radio talk show. On the radio program, Billy reveals his having been kidnapped by Tralfamadorians and taken to their planet, Tralfamadore. Held in a zoo by the Tralfamadorians, Billy mated with Montana Wildhack, a pornographic movie star from Earth, while his captors watched. In the novel, events in Billy's life come and go in no particular order; his pilgrimage is written in no strict chronology.

The most important happenings in Billy's life related in Chapter Two concern his World War II experiences. A summary of these army experiences leads to Billy's first encounter with time tripping. During his early military training, Billy becomes a chaplain's assistant. While on maneuvers in South Carolina, he is granted a furlough to attend his father's funeral in Ilium. His father has been accidentally shot while deer hunting. After the funeral, Billy is sent overseas and assigned to replace a chaplain's assistant killed in action.

When he joins his unit in Luxembourg, the regiment is under attack by German forces. The enemy attack creates a great deal of chaos and leaves many, including Billy, dazed and wandering behind German lines. With Billy are three others: two regimental scouts and Roland Weary, an antitank gunner. All are hopelessly lost, without food or maps.

Billy's group wanders for three days in the snow and cold under constant sniper fire. Weary constantly prods Billy to keep up and not fall behind. Raised in a family that idolizes weapons of torture, Weary fantasizes that he and the two scouts are the Three Musketeers.

During one of the times when Billy lags far behind the others, he comes *unstuck in time*; the rest of the group remain *stuck*. He fast-forwards to the time of his death before traveling backwards to a time before his birth. Next, he moves forward again and stops at a point when he is a child. He then travels to the year 1965 and visits the nursing home in which he has placed his mother. The next time trip takes him briefly to a banquet honoring his son Robert's Little League team. Suddenly, it is New Year's Eve, 1961, and he finds himself extremely drunk and removing a woman's girdle at a party of optometrists. He passes out.

When Billy regains consciousness, he is back in 1944. Weary is shaking him, urging him to move forward. Although Billy pleads to be left behind, Weary insists on saving him. The scouts grow tired of Billy and Weary's wrangling and desert them, after which Billy travels in time and finds himself at a lectern in a restaurant, receiving an ovation from the Ilium, New York, Lions Club: He has been elected president of the club, which is ironic given that his passive actions throughout the novel demonstrate that he is anything *but* a lion. He again returns to World War II just as he and Weary are being captured by German soldiers.

Commentary

At the beginning of this chapter, a rapid series of brief, biographical events is presented in strict chronology. This chronology of these events is contrasted with Billy's coming unstuck in time in 1944, in a German forest, leaping in and out of the future and the past. The randomness of the events suggests that free will has no effect on the ordering: Billy cannot choose the sequence; he must experience the events as they happen. The interplay of past and future scenes occurs according to a predetermined pattern, although it is unclear who or what determines what that pattern will be, or when it will happen.

On Earth, time is chronological, linear. One moment follows another like beads on a string. But the Tralfamadorian concept of time is that all events exist simultaneously. If a person views all time simultaneously, that person will have knowledge of all events. Godlike, the Tralfamadorians seem to have transcended impermanence, never dying; they possess a capacity of omnipotence. Likewise, Billy, a prophet of the Tralfamadorian gospel, seems to be approaching a state of omnipotence. But no one, except the science-fiction writer Kilgore Trout, takes him seriously. Billy's daughter, Barbara, threatens to put him in a mental institution; on a radio talk show in New York City, he is ejected from the studios for his views.

During his ordeal behind enemy lines, Billy is often near death. According to Weary, the Three Musketeers—Weary and the two scouts—save Billy's life again and again. Billy's salvation in Luxembourg is but a preview of his ultimate salvation when he is executed in Chicago. After all, according to Tralfamadorian philosophy, all events, including death, are equally meaningful. Therefore, death is not an end in itself: Death is simply one more event in a person's life to be lived and relived again and again.

• **Lake Placid**   a village in northeast New York in the Adirondack Mountains; site of the Winter Olympics in 1932 and 1980.

- **the Green Berets**   members of a U.S. Army Special Forces outfit known for their heroic deeds during wartime; an elite troop of soldiers trained in counterinsurgency and guerrilla warfare.

- **Vietnam**   A country in southeast Asia, it was partitioned into North Vietnam and South Vietnam after 1954, and reunited in 1976 after the end of the Vietnam War (1954–75).

- **carbon-monoxide poisoning**   Colorless and odorless, carbon monoxide (CO) is a highly poisonous gas formed by the incomplete combustion of carbonaceous material, such as gasoline.

- **rumpus room**   a room for plays and parties, often in the basement of a house or building.

- **cockles**   idiomatically, one's innermost feelings.

- **flibbertigibbet**   a silly or scatterbrained person.

- *vox humana*   Latin, meaning "human voice."

- *vox celeste*   Latin, meaning "celestial voice."

- **Johann Sebastian Bach**   (1685–1750) German composer and organist of the late baroque period.

- **Martin Luther**   (1483–1546) German theologian and leader of the Reformation.

- **Luxembourg**   a country in northwest Europe; created as a duchy in 1354 and declared a neutral territory in 1867.

- **the Battle of the Bulge**   the last German offensive on the Western Front during World War II, occurring between December 16, 1944, and January 16, 1945, in the Ardennes region of southern Belgium; "Bulge" refers to the wedge that the Germans drove into the Allied lines before being repulsed back.

- **Indian file**   single file.

- **Colt .45 automatic**   the popular name of the .45 caliber Colt U.S. Army M1911 A1 semiautomatic pistol; named for Samuel Colt (1814–62), the American firearms inventor who developed the first revolver.

- **Tiger tank**   a heavily armored tank, weighing 56 tons and mounting a long 88-mm. gun, used by the Germans during World War II.

- **Spanish thumbscrew**   an instrument of torture used to compress the thumb, causing extreme pain.

- **dum-dums**   hollow-point small-arms bullets designed to expand upon impact, inflicting gaping wounds.

- **derringer pistol**   a small, short-barreled pistol that has a large bore; named for Henry Derringer (1786–1868), an American gunsmith.

- **the Great Depression**   the period of drastic decline in the U.S. economy from 1929 to 1940; immortalized in John Steinbeck's *The Grapes of Wrath* (1939).

- **Shetland pony**   a small pony originating in the Shetland Islands, in northern Scotland.

- **deedlee-balls**   small balls usually made from yarn; often used as accessory decorations.

- **Doric columns**   heavy columns with plain, saucer-shaped capitals and no base.

- **Tuileries Gardens**   the public gardens located in the center of Paris and designed for Louis XIV.

- **The Three Musketeers**   the three main characters (Athos, Porthos, and Aramis) in Alexandre Dumas' French historical romance *The Three Musketeers* (1844).

- **Bronze Star**   a U.S. military decoration awarded either for heroism or for meritorious achievement in ground combat.

- **the Parthenon**   the chief temple of the goddess Athena, built on the Acropolis at Athens between 447 and 432 B.C.

- **the Lions Club**   a service club organization founded in Dallas, Texas, in 1917, with member clubs throughout the U.S.

CHAPTER THREE

Summary

Assigned the duty of rounding up lost or wounded Americans, the German soldiers who capture Billy and Weary include two boys in their early teens, two tattered, old men, and a middle-aged corporal who has been wounded four times and is sick of war. Billy's attention is drawn to the corporal's boots. Polished and pure looking, they remind Billy of the innocence and purity of Adam and Eve: Billy loves them. Standing next to the old corporal is a fifteen-year-old blond boy wearing wooden clogs. To Billy, the boy seems to be an angel. From some distance they hear shots. The two scouts who abandoned Billy and Weary have been discovered by other German soldiers and are shot. They now lie dying in the snow.

After searching Billy for weapons and taking Weary's pistol, trench knife, bulletproof Bible, and his pornographic picture of a woman and a pony, the German soldiers force Weary to give his boots to the fifteen-year-old boy. Billy and Weary are then taken to a cottage that serves as a collecting point for captured American soldiers.

Time traveling once again, Billy finds himself in his Ilium optometry office in 1967. He has trouble treating his patients, and he worries about his mental condition in general. Struggling to recall his age, he tries to remember what year it is but has no idea. Because he is terrified at the thought of another war, he is easily alarmed when he hears what he thinks is a siren, but it is only the noon-day whistle sounding from the firehouse across the street.

Billy closes his eyes and briefly returns to 1944 Luxembourg. He is being photographed by a German war correspondent, who will use the snapshot as propaganda, showing how poorly equipped the American army is. The guards throw Billy into some bushes, and his picture is taken as he emerges with Germans wielding their weapons.

Billy comes unstuck in time and again trips ahead to 1967. On a hot August day, he is driving to a Lions Club luncheon in Ilium. The speaker at the luncheon, a Marine Corps major, implores the audience to keep supporting the war in Vietnam until a victory is won, or until the Communists learn that they cannot impose their ways on others. The major is introduced to Billy and tells him that he should be proud of his son, Robert, a Green Beret fighting in Vietnam. Leaving the luncheon, Billy goes home for his daily nap, but sleep does not come. Instead, he begins to weep.

When he opens his eyes, he is still weeping, but now he is again back in Luxembourg, and it is the winter wind that brings tears to his eyes. Billy and his fellow American prisoners are forcibly marched into Germany, a march that Billy unexpectedly finds exciting. At sundown, they reach a railroad yard with rows of waiting boxcars; sorted according to rank, they are crammed inside. Pushed into a corner next to a ventilator, Billy is able to see outside.

Although their train does not budge for two days, the prisoners are not allowed to get out of the boxcars. Through the ventilators, they are given water, loaves of black bread, sausage, and cheese. They relieve themselves by excreting into steel helmets and passing the helmets to people at the ventilators, who dump them outside. Billy is a dumper.

On Christmas Eve, the train gets underway at last and begins to creep eastward. That night, Billy comes unstuck in time and travels to the night when he is kidnapped by Tralfamadorians.

Commentary

Vonnegut's description of the blond German boy's feet being swaddled in rags alludes to the story of the birth of Christ, in which Mary wraps the baby in swaddling clothes. Such comparisons, often casting Billy in the role of a Christ-figure, are made throughout *Slaughterhouse-Five*. Both Billy's last name, Pilgrim, and the subtitle of the novel suggest that Billy is on a spiritual pilgrimage. Textually, the pilgrimage begins when Vonnegut foreshadows Billy as a Christ-figure in the epigraph. And just as Christ serves as an eternal role model for Christians, Billy becomes eternal because he will live on, according to Tralfamadorian philosophy, through the cyclical events of his life. Ultimately, he will be executed by a sniper, but Christ-like, he will not succumb to the finality of death in linear time; instead, he will endure in the never-ending cycle of psychological time.

The description of the dead scouts' blood turning the snow the color of raspberry sherbet demonstrates a verbal indifference to the act of death and recalls the distancing effect in the expression *So it goes*. Raspberry sherbet is a mild description for human blood, but the image foreshadows many acts of indifference demonstrated throughout *Slaughterhouse-Five*. Despite the destruction he has seen in World War II, Billy is not aroused to protest the bombing of North Vietnam when he hears the Marine Corps major suggest bombing the country "back to the Stone Age."

Billy's avoidance of obligation is made paramount once again. When he observes a pair of disabled men selling bogus magazine subscriptions, he neither calls the police nor answers the door. Instead, he closes his eyes and simply ignores the matter. His passivity emphasizes the theme of predestination: Because he cannot alter the forces shaping his life, he chooses not to try.

The panorama of war tantalizes his imagination. The image he beholds of blue and ivory frozen feet invokes a state of paralysis that will become manifest in others. Later, Vonnegut will carry these color allusions to an even greater extent. Images of blue and ivory, denoting desolation, sterility, and disability, are used extensively throughout *Slaughterhouse-Five*.

- **Ausable Chasm** Located in northeast New York, the chasm was caused by the plunging Ausable River, creating spectacular waterfalls, rushing rapids, and fantastic rock formations.

- **Earl Warren** (1891–1974) chief justice of the U.S. Supreme Court from 1953 to 1969, during which time the Court ruled on many social issues, including civil rights.

- **John Birch Society** an ultra-conservative organization founded by Robert H. W. Welch, Jr., in 1958, and named for a U.S. intelligence officer killed by Chinese Communists soon after the end of World War II.

- **Leica** an expensive German camera introduced in 1924 and still manufactured today; known for the quality not only of the camera itself, but also for its excellent lenses.

- **Croesus** the last king of Lydia (560–546 B.C.), an ancient and Roman province in southwest Asia Minor on the Aegean Sea; slang for a wealthy man.

- *fourragère* an ornamental braided cord usually looped around the left shoulder of a uniform.

- **double pneumonia** an acute or chronic disease marked by the inflammation of both lungs.

- **vertigo** the sensation of dizziness often caused by the fear of heights.

- **cannonball stove** also referred to as a cannon stove; a round, cast-iron stove, hence the term "cannonball."

CHAPTER FOUR

Summary

On the night of his daughter's wedding, Billy is kidnapped by Tralfamadorians. Prior to this event, he notes several things that remind him of his World War II experiences: the orange-and-black canopy in his backyard under which Barbara is married; his blue-

and-ivory feet; and an old war movie that he watches forwards and backwards. Communicating telepathically, Billy and his captors discuss the significance of his being chosen by the Tralfamadorians: Quite simply, there is none. After the aliens prepare him for interstellar flight, the tremendous acceleration of the saucer sends him back to World War II.

Still in the boxcar, he travels across Germany. The train stops at various prison camps to drop off POWs. On the ninth day of traveling, Roland Weary dies. He has been raving for some time, speaking of the Three Musketeers and leaving messages for his family back home. He yearns to be avenged, and again and again in his delirium, Weary divulges the name of the person who killed him: Billy Pilgrim.

On the tenth night, the train arrives at a prison camp, and guards force the prisoners out of the boxcars. Issued overcoats, they shuffle through gate after gate until they arrive at a delousing station and are ordered to take off their clothes and be deloused. The narrator describes two of the prisoners: Edgar Derby, a former high school teacher in Indianapolis, and Paul Lazzaro, who was in the same boxcar with Weary and promised him that he would make Billy pay for Weary's death.

Billy comes unstuck in time again. He is an infant, then a middle-aged man playing golf, and then he is onboard a flying saucer headed for the planet Tralfamadore. A loudspeaker on the spacecraft explains that Tralfamadorians understand time differently than do humans. A Tralfamadorian sees all time as an Earthling might see a stretch of mountains. Time is simply time. It does not change, nor does it lend itself to explanation: It simply is. When Billy suggests that Tralfamadorians do not appear to believe in free will, he is told that free will is an Earthling's notion; out of more than one hundred inhabited planets, only Earth's inhabitants talk about free will.

Commentary

The orange-and-black tent used for Barbara's wedding ceremony recalls the orange-and-black banners on the train transporting the POWs. In Chapter Three, we were told that orange and black indicated a train that was not fair game for air attack. Using the same analogy, orange-and-black stripes on the tent may suggest that the bride is no longer free to date socially, that she is off-limits to men other than her husband. But more in the tenor of the narrative is the implication that the institution of marriage is akin to the incarceration of a POW camp and the prison of conformity in which Billy lives.

Once again, the colors blue and ivory are used to describe Billy's feet. The report on the condition of Billy's feet immediately follows a brief description of his wife Valencia's reproductive state. Valencia has undergone a hysterectomy and is now infertile. These depictions of stasis, or stoppage, appear only a few pages after a description of the Americans standing naked in the POW camp's delousing shower. Their genitalia are rendered impotent by the paralysis of their predicament—the POWs are disabled, powerless to exercise free will. Although these episodes are separated by more than twenty years in linear time, they connect closely in terms of psychological time, a connection that is established again and again in *Slaughterhouse-Five*.

Billy watches the World War II movie forwards; then he watches it backwards. Seeing it backwards removes any suspense about the outcome. He experiences the effect of predestination: Because events in the future are known before they occur, free will is nonexistent. The significance of predestination is found in his questioning the Tralfamadorians why *he* has been chosen. "Why *you?*" they condescendingly ask him. "Why *anything?*" Moments in time simply *are*: "There is no *why*."

The notion of predestination also concerns Edgar Derby, who serves as a figure of contradictions. As a high school educator, he taught a course called "Contemporary Problems in Western Civilization." Now a soldier in Europe, Derby is presented literally with a contemporary problem of Western civilization. The irony is that, through the exercise of free will, the study of a problem should yield a solution. Yet despite attempts in the application of free will, humankind seemingly finds itself the slave of predestination.

- **bandsaw**   a power saw for woodworking, consisting of a toothed metal band coupled to and driven around two wheels.

- **Barca-Lounger**   an upholstered lounge chair similar to a La-Z-Boy recliner.

- **madrigal**   an unaccompanied vocal composition for two or three voices.

34

- **Sir Isaac Newton** (1642–1727) English scientist who invented differential calculus and formulated the theory of universal gravitation.

- **delousing** to get rid of lice by physical or chemical means.

CHAPTER FIVE

Summary

On the trip to Tralfamadore, Billy asks for something to read. After reading the only Earthling novel onboard, he is given some Tralfamadorian books. Unable to read the alien language, he is surprised that the books' tiny text is laid out in brief knots of symbols separated by stars. He is told that the clumps of symbols are like telegrams—short, urgent messages. Tralfamadorians read them all at once, not one after the other; there is no beginning, no middle, no end. There are no causes, no effects.

As the saucer enters a time warp, Billy is hurled back into his childhood: He is twelve years old. With his father and mother, he is visiting the Grand Canyon. Jumping ahead ten more days, he is still with his family on the same trip, only now they are in the bowels of Carlsbad Caverns. Billy prays for God to deliver him before the ceiling collapses.

Suddenly, he finds himself back in 1945 Germany. He and his fellow POWs are marched to a shed, where a one-armed, one-eyed corporal writes their names and serial numbers in a ledger. Now the prisoners are legally alive—moments before, they were missing in action. Following a quarrel between a guard who understands English and an American who mutters some offensive remark, each prisoner is given a dog tag with a number stamped on it. The tag is perforated through the center: In case of death it can be snapped in two—one part to mark the corpse, the other to mark the grave. Billy and his fellow prisoners are housed with a group of fifty spirited Englishmen, who have been imprisoned for four years.

That night in the Englishmen's compound, a musical version of *Cinderella* is performed by the English officers. Watching it, Billy begins to laugh hysterically, then he begins to shriek. He continues shrieking until he is carried out of the shed to the hospital, where he is tied down in bed and given a shot of morphine.

The morphine triggers another time trip, this time to spring 1948. Billy finds himself in a New York veterans' hospital, where he has voluntarily committed himself to a ward for nonviolent mental patients. In the bed next to Billy is a former infantry captain named Eliot Rosewater, who introduces Billy to the science-fiction novels of Kilgore Trout. Billy and Rosewater have one thing in common— both have found life meaningless and are trying to come to grips with the horrors of World War II. During the war, Rosewater mistook a fourteen-year-old fireman for a German soldier and shot him. Billy experienced the senseless destruction of life during the fire bombing of Dresden. Science fiction is a tool that Billy and Rosewater both use to reconstruct themselves and their universe.

In a split second, Billy is flung back to 1945 before being hurled ahead once more to the veterans' hospital. Billy's mother is visiting him; when she leaves, Valencia Merble, Billy's fiancée, sits with him. Drawn into their conversation, Rosewater tells them that he is reading a Kilgore Trout novel, *The Gospel from Outer Space*, about an alien who visits Earth and writes a new Gospel. In the new Gospel, Jesus is not the Son of God, yet people still decide to lynch this nobody.

Billy time trips again, and this time he travels to the Tralfamadore zoo, where he is confined in a geodesic dome. Outside the dome, thousands of Tralfamadorians observe him. Naked, Billy goes through the regimen of eating, washing the dishes, and putting them away; he does a series of exercises; he shaves, trims his toenails, and sprays deodorant under his arms. Outside, a guide lectures telepathically to the crowd. When one of the spectators asks Billy if he is happy on Tralfamadore, he answers that he is about as happy as he was on Earth.

Billy is surprised to learn that the Tralfamadorians are not alarmed by the acts of murder and war carried out on Earth. Asked about the most valuable thing he has learned on Tralfamadore, he replies that it is how the inhabitants of an entire planet can live together in peace. In soaring elocution, he describes the murder and mayhem that take place on Earth, and he concludes by suggesting that this mass behavior will surely be a threat to the future of the universe. But the Tralfamadorians find him ignorant: They know how the universe will end, and madness and violence on Earth have nothing to do with it. The universe will be blown up by a Tralfamadorian conducting experiments with flying-saucer fuel. When Billy asks if there is not some way to prevent this destruction, he is told that there is not: The future is simply structured this way.

Battleground Map of

The Battle of the Bulge

This last, major German military offensive of World War II took place in December 1944 and January 1945 in the Ardennes, a densely forested region of rugged terrain running from Belgium southward into Luxembourg. Hitler's aim was to cross the Meuse River and recapture Brussels and Antwerp. The Germans numbered 275,000 troops and nearly 1000 armored vehicles. Defending the 60-mile western front from Monschau to Echternach were 83,000 Americans and only 420 armored vehicles.

On December 16, the Germans attacked the greatly outnumbered southern flank of the American line, which was forced back. In the north, American troops retreated. On December 17, the Germans engulfed Bastogne—which American troops defended masterfully—and continued westward. By December 18, a "bulge" had been created in the Ardennes, but the German forces were running out of momentum. Western Allied reinforcements were brought in, and by December 26, they had broken through German lines to relieve Bastogne, while other Western Allied forces advanced from the north. On January 15, Western Allied forces continued marching eastward, eventually reestablishing the front line remarkably similar to that prior to the German offensive.

LEGEND
— U.S. front line, Dec. 15, 1944
--- U.S. front line, Dec. 24, 1944
····· U.S. front line, Feb. 7, 1945

The Battle of the Bulge

In *Slaughterhouse-Five,* Billy Pilgrim fights in the Battle of the Bulge, is lost behind German lines, and is captured. He is first sent to a prison camp in the Chemnitz area, and eventually to Dresden.

Slaughterhouse-Five

World War II Europe

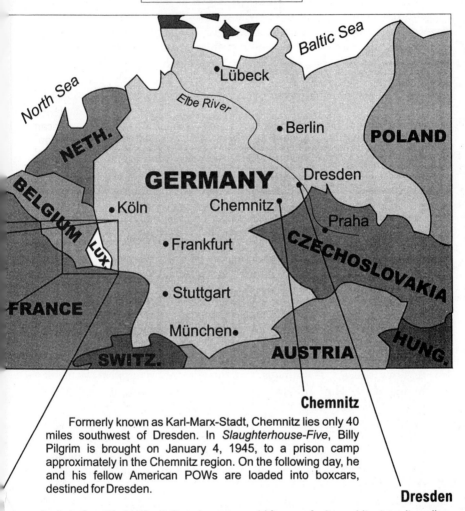

Chemnitz

Formerly known as Karl-Marx-Stadt, Chemnitz lies only 40 miles southwest of Dresden. In *Slaughterhouse-Five*, Billy Pilgrim is brought on January 4, 1945, to a prison camp approximately in the Chemnitz region. On the following day, he and his fellow American POWs are loaded into boxcars, destined for Dresden.

Dresden

Long before World War II, Dresden was world famous for its architecture, its collections of priceless art, and its china industry. Near the end of World War II, it was the site of massive Western Allied bombing from February 13, 1945, to April 17, 1945. Death figures range from 35,000 up to 135,000, mostly civilians. The bombing operation remains controversial, with some critics arguing that Dresden's destruction was militarily unnecessary, and others claiming that the city housed a vital communications center. Today, Dresden has a population of 525,000, and much of the city has been rebuilt.

In *Slaughterhouse-Five*, Billy Pilgrim arrives in Dresden on January 5, 1945, 39 days prior to the first bombing run. Eventually, Russian Allies gain control of Dresden, and Billy is turned over to American forces and shipped home.

Falling asleep that night, Billy travels back to Ilium. He has been out of the mental hospital for six months; he has graduated from the Ilium School of Optometry—which is ironic given that he now prescribes corrective lenses for people with defective physical vision, yet no one understands his own philosophical vision of the world; and he has just married Valencia Merble. The night of their wedding, Billy travels through a series of experiences: to the prison hospital, to his father's funeral, back to the prison hospital, to 1968 and his being reproached by his daughter, Barbara, and to the Tralfamadore zoo.

The Tralfamadorians furnish Billy with a mate named Montana Wildhack, a pornographic motion picture star on Earth. He makes no attempts to entice her affections, but within a week she asks him to sleep with her. After Billy makes love to Montana, he travels through time and space back to his home in Ilium.

Commentary

Two instances of Vonnegut's commenting on his own writing are presented in this chapter—first, Billy talks about the Tralfamadorian books, and second, Eliot Rosewater offers his opinions about Kilgore Trout's writing.

Onboard the flying saucer, Billy puzzles over the Tralfamadorian books laid out in brief knots of symbols separated by stars. He is told that the clumps of symbols are like telegrams—short, urgent messages; Tralfamadorians read the messages all at once, not in sequence. The Tralfamadorian concept of writing is similar to that which Vonnegut proposes in Chapter One. Billy's story in *Slaughterhouse-Five* has no beginning, no middle, no end, just as Tralfamadorian writing has none. No suspense occurs in the novel because Vonnegut divulges all of Billy's life by the end of Chapter Two, just as all of the past, the present, and the future is known to the Tralfamadorians.

Because much of Vonnegut's writing questions the validity of authority, he is careful not to set himself up as an authority on any subject, not even his own writing. When Rosewater tells Billy that Trout's writing is frightful, we understand that Vonnegut is comparing himself to Trout: Any comments made about Trout as a writer also extend to Vonnegut since he, too, is a writer of little-known, philosophical novels.

The nature of time is again a primary theme in this chapter, as it has been throughout the preceding chapter. When a park ranger turns out the lights deep inside Carlsbad Caverns, Billy questions his state of being. Deep inside the dark caverns, the ghostly iridescence of the dial on Billy's father's watch serves as a reminder of the dichotomy between linear and psychological time. The watch displaces the events of psychological time and brings back the world of authoritarian reality in chronological time. The limitations of chronological time are similar to the limitations of humans' three-dimensional vision, described in terms of Billy's perspective. Using the metaphor of looking through a pipe, we realize that three-dimensional vision is like being able to see only a speck at the end of the pipe. Only Tralfamadorians have the benefit of four-dimensional vision: They see everything at once, while Billy sees only what is in front of him.

In the Tralfamadore zoo, Billy is the focus of observation, just as he is in the Dresden parade of prisoners. On Tralfamadore, he is estranged because he is a naked alien. In the Dresden camp, he is estranged because of the clownish overcoat he is given to wear: The ragged coat has a fur collar that makes him look like a clown and causes guards and prisoners alike to laugh. The comparisons between Billy's experiences on Tralfamadore and those in the Dresden camp heighten the novel's satire. The horror of his ordeal during World War II is related to the horror of his being kidnapped by space aliens. His captivity on Tralfamadore happens on a fantasy level and is comical, which serves to make his World War II captivity seem far worse because it occurs on a realistic level.

- **millipedes**   insects with long, segmented bodies and two pairs of legs attached to each segment; when they scurry across a surface, they look as if they have a thousand legs.

- **Carlsbad Caverns**   a group of limestone caverns in the Guadalupe Mountains of southeast New Mexico.

- *Pirates of Penzance*   A comic opera with lyrics by W. S. Gilbert and music by Arthur Sullivan, it debuted in London on April 3, 1880.

- **croquet**   an outdoor game in which players, using long-handled mallets, drive wooden balls through a series of wickets.

- **Jerry**   a German soldier.

- *The Red Badge of Courage* Stephen Crane's 1895 novel about the American Civil War, depicting the psychological turmoil of a cowardly soldier in combat.

- **morphine** a drug extracted from opium and generally used as a sedative.

- *The Brothers Karamazov* Written by the Russian novelist Fyodor Dostoyevsky and first published between 1879 and 1880, this novel addresses one dysfunctional family's search for values and unity.

- **WACS** Women's Army Corp.

- **WAVES** Women Appointed for Voluntary Emergency Service.

- **SPARS** Women's Reserve of the U.S. Coast Guard; derived from the U.S. Coast Guard's motto, *Semper Paratus*, meaning "Always Prepared."

- **WAFS** Women's Auxiliary Ferrying Squadron.

- **William Blake** (1757–1827) English poet and engraver, perhaps best known for his book of poems *Songs of Innocence and Experience* (1794).

- **Dunkirk** a city in northwest France on the North Sea; in World War II, more than 330,000 Allied troops were evacuated from its beaches in the face of enemy fire (May–June 1940).

- **Gay Nineties** the 1890s, an era characterized by a carefree attitude, that all's right with the world.

- **Queen Elizabeth the First** (1533–1603) Queen of England and Ireland (1558–1603) who reestablished Protestantism in England.

- **Indian Summer** a period of mild weather occurring in late autumn.

- **French doors** a pair of doors of light construction, with glass panes extending for most of their length.

- **the battle for Hill 875 near Dakto** a battle during the Vietnam War beginning November 3, 1967, and lasting twenty-two days.

CHAPTER SIX

Summary

Billy wakes up in the prison camp hospital. Both Paul Lazzaro and Edgar Derby are nearby. Lazzaro explains that he holds Billy responsible for the death of Roland Weary. He also divulges a promise he made to Weary—he will kill Billy. He tells Billy to enjoy life while he can.

As a time traveler, Billy knows that Lazzaro's threat will come to pass. Billy has seen his death many times and has described it on a tape recorder he keeps in a safe deposit box. The tape recorder's message is: *"I, Billy Pilgrim, will die, have died, and always will die on February thirteenth, 1976."* Billy says that at the time of his death, he will be speaking at an engagement in Chicago on the nature of time and flying saucers. As he lectures to the large crowd, he predicts his death—within an hour—revealing Lazzaro's promise to kill him. He closes his speech with a message that death is not eternal. As Billy leaves the stage, a sniper fires at him from the press box. Billy Pilgrim is dead.

Billy time travels to 1945 Germany. Having left the POW hospital, he listens as an English officer lectures the Americans on personal hygiene. The officer reproaches them for their apparent lack of survival instincts and tells them it is important that they take pride in their appearance. Informing the Americans that they will be leaving the prison camp that very afternoon for Dresden, the English officer describes Dresden as an open city: It is undefended and contains no war industries or troop concentrations. In Dresden, they need not worry about being bombed.

The American prisoners march out of the compound headed for Dresden, with Edgar Derby and Billy at the head of the column. Derby has been elected leader. Billy wears a pair of silver boots he has found, and draped around him like a toga are some azure curtains taken from the Englishmen's compound; his hands are wrapped in the tiny, fur-collared coat that he carries like a muff.

At the railroad yard, the Americans board four boxcars. The trip to Dresden takes only two hours. A magnificent city, the loveliest the Americans have ever seen, Dresden is the only large German city exempt from Allied bombing. Although air raid sirens go off every day and the people go into their cellars, the planes overhead are always headed for other targets. In Dresden, life goes on in a civilized fashion: streetcars run, telephones work, and electrical power for lighting is functional. Theaters and restaurants are in service, and there is a zoo.

The boxcars carrying the American prisoners are met by a squad of eight German soldiers. Two of the guards are veterans who were badly wounded on the eastern front. The other six, boys and elderly men, were sworn into the army just the day before. One of the men has an artificial leg and carries a rifle and a cane. When the Americans climb down, the guards' apprehensions vanish and they begin to laugh. They have nothing to fear: The Americans are nothing more than disabled buffoons like themselves.

Out of the gates of the railroad yard and into the streets of the city march the eight guards and their American prisoners. Thousands of tired townspeople on their way home after work are entertained by the parade. Billy is unaware of the ridiculous impression he presents, unaware of how this spectacle of misfits must look to other people. His mind is elsewhere: His memory of the future reminds him that the city will be bombed in about a month, and that most of the people watching this parade of American prisoners will be killed. Walking through the streets, Billy is mesmerized by the general beauty of the city, especially its architecture. As he trudges along, his fingers fondle two lumps he feels in the lining of his muff.

While stopped at a red light, he is addressed by an English-speaking German who takes affront to Billy's insufferable attire. The German assumes that Billy purposefully selected his costume. Billy is stunned by the German's questions. In his feeble attempt to be benevolent, he grasps the two objects in the lining of his coat. He reaches out and holds them under the German's nose: On his palm lie a two-carat diamond and a partial denture.

The procession staggers along until it reaches the inoperative Dresden stockyards, where the men are taken to a cement-block building formerly used to house hogs. Inside, they find bunks, stoves, and a water tap. Outside, there is a makeshift latrine. Over the door a number has been painted: number five. A guard tells them to memorize their new address in case they get lost: *Schlachthof-fünf*—Slaughterhouse-five.

Commentary

Billy does not object when he learns that he will be murdered by an assassin's bullet. His contact with Tralfamadorians has taught him the meaning of predestination. He knows he will die on a particular date in 1976, yet he is aware that death is only one event in life, and that he will travel to other events in the future and in the past.

Once again, Edgar Derby demonstrates the personification of

irony. In Chapter Four, we learned that Derby taught "Contemporary Problems in Western Civilization," and yet, ironically, he is personally enveloped in war, one of the greatest problems of our time, and is at the mercy of his captors. In this chapter, a letter he composes to his wife just before being led out of the POW camp is another comment on the pathetic irony linked to his character. He writes that he is going to Dresden, and that his wife should not worry as Dresden will never be bombed. Of course, it will be.

The colors of stasis, blue and ivory, appear once again. As the prisoners return to the railhead, they see the body of the hobo who rode initially with them to the POW camp, but who died along the way. The hobo's corpse, its feet blue and ivory, lies where the Germans left it. For the hobo, death is the final condition of paralysis, a final statement concerning his ability to exercise free will.

- **Golgotha**   a hill outside ancient Jerusalem, where Jesus was crucified; also known as Calvary.

- **Balkanized**   a term originally referring to the political division of the Balkans in the early twentieth century; today, it means dividing a region or territory into small units.

- **"The Spirit of '76"**   an 1876 oil painting by Archibald MacNeal Willard (1836–1918), called "Yankee Doodle"; it captures the fighting qualities of the colonial troops in the three main figures, two drummers and a fife player.

- **Leipzig, Chemnitz, Plauen**   all cities located in east-central Germany, southwest of Berlin.

- **potbellied stove**   a short, rounded, usually freestanding stove, in which wood or coal is burned.

CHAPTER SEVEN

Summary

Twenty-five years after the bombing of Dresden, Billy boards an airplane in Ilium, New York, chartered to carry him, his father-in-law, Lionel Merble, and nearly thirty other optometrists to a convention in Montreal, Canada. Billy knows the airplane will crash, but he says nothing. The passengers are entertained by a barbershop quartet. The group sings lewd, racist songs to entertain Billy's father-in-law. Merble laughs heartily: He begs the quartet to sing a second ethnic-degrading song, one he regards highly.

When the plane crashes into Sugarbush Mountain, Vermont, everyone is killed—except Billy and the copilot. First to arrive at the wreckage are Austrian ski instructors from the Sugarbush Ski School. Speaking in German, the ski instructors move quickly from body to body. As one of the ski instructors bends over Billy to hear his dying words, Billy whispers, "Schlachthof-fünf." Taken to a small hospital, where a brain surgeon operates on him, he lies unconscious for two days, experiencing a multiplicity of dreams.

Billy finds himself in 1945 Dresden. He and Edgar Derby, sent to fetch supper for their fellow prisoners, are guarded by sixteen-year-old Werner Gluck. Leading the way to a building that he thinks is the kitchen, Gluck discovers a dressing room and a communal shower. Inside are thirty teen-age girls—refugees from the city of Breslau who have just arrived in Dresden. Standing in the nude, the girls find themselves under the examining eyes of the teenage Werner Gluck, the tired, old Edgar Derby, and the clownish Billy Pilgrim. The girls scream and cover themselves with their hands as best they can. Neither Gluck nor Billy has ever seen a naked woman before. They eventually locate the kitchen.

During their stay in the converted slaughterhouse, the prisoners are assigned a variety of daily duties. They wash windows, sweep floors, and clean toilets in a factory that makes malt syrup enriched with vitamins and minerals for pregnant women. They also pack jars of the malt syrup in boxes.

Throughout the day many of the workers filch spoonfuls of the syrup. Spoons are hidden all over the plant. On his second day, Billy discovers a spoon. He uses the spoon to taste the syrup, then passes the syrup-covered spoon to Derby, who is standing outside a window watching Billy. Derby bursts into tears.

Commentary

The doomed plane trip on which Billy's father-in-law dies allows Vonnegut to explore once again the theme of predestination. Although Billy knows that the plane will crash, and that everyone but the copilot and himself will die, he says nothing to avert the disaster: He cannot change the series of events that is his life.

Slaughterhouse-Five is replete with sexist, racist language, as exemplified by Lionel Merble and the barbershop quartet. The barbershop quartet's singing vulgar songs calls attention to the transgressions among many everyday people. The degrading songs that Merble and the quartet so enjoy emphasize the point that no character is totally good. However, no character is all bad, either. After all, despite Merble's fondness for the lewd songs, he has helped establish Billy in his profession. Also, Vonnegut might be hinting at the theme of passivity—which certainly has affected Billy's life—a notion recalling various charges against German citizens who were thought to have passively condoned the Nazis' actions during World War II.

The mention of the vitamin- and mineral-enriched syrup manufactured for pregnant women serves the ongoing theme of irony. The malt syrup is made to strengthen women and to nurture babies that are yet to be born. The life-sustaining syrup is a positive symbol of the human condition surrounded by the chaos and massacre of war. Bringing forth life in an environment that will soon be destroyed is a potent example of the novel's irony. Also, note that Edgar Derby is associated with this example of irony, just as he has been throughout the novel.

- **Elbe River**   a major European river flowing through Germany, including the city of Dresden, and the Czech Republic.

- **Breslau**   also known as Wroclaw, a city in southwest Poland; assigned to Poland by the Potsdam Conference.

CHAPTER EIGHT

Summary

Two days before Dresden is bombed, the American prisoners are visited by Howard W. Campbell, Jr., an American Nazi. The author of propaganda about the demeanor of American prisoners of war, Campbell has come to the food processing facility to recruit volunteers for a new German military organization, "The Free American Corps," whose purpose is to fight against the Russians.

Outfitted in an outrageous uniform, including a white ten-gallon hat, a blue body stocking with yellow stripes reaching from armpit to ankle, and a red arm band with a blue swastika in a circle of white, Campbell offers the prisoners a full meal of steak and potatoes if they will join his organization. He tells them that they will be repatriated once the Russians are defeated.

At first there is no response, but then Edgar Derby hauls himself to his feet and declares that Campbell is lower than a blood-filled tick. Inspired, Derby speaks about freedom, justice, and fair play. He talks of a brotherhood between Americans and Russians, telling Campbell how the two nations will crush "the disease of Nazism."

Disrupted by the sound of air raid sirens, everyone takes shelter in a meat locker deep beneath the slaughterhouse. Bombs are not dropped on Dresden that night, but the prisoners and their guards remain underground. As Billy falls asleep in the meat locker, he travels to Ilium.

Billy describes meeting Kilgore Trout, the science-fiction writer who also lives in Ilium. Because he has never made any money as a writer, Trout works in the circulation department for the *Ilium Gazette*, supervising newspaper delivery boys. When Billy meets him, Trout is haggling with dozens of his delivery boys. Billy helps Trout deliver papers and invites him to a party celebrating his and Valencia's eighteenth wedding anniversary.

At the anniversary party, the barbershop quartet that will later sing on the ill-fated chartered plane to Montreal performs. Their singing arouses a distressing response in Billy. He looks so strange that several of the guests conclude that he is suffering a heart attack. Trout asks Billy if he has seen through time—many of Trout's novels deal with time travel—and Billy denies that he has. When the barbershop quartet strikes up another song, he is overcome once again. Escaping upstairs, he ponders the effect the men in the quartet have on him and remembers the first night of the Dresden bombing.

Billy and the prisoners are still deep underground in the meat locker. From above they feel the concussion of bombs. When they emerge the following day, the sky is black with smoke. The city looks like the surface of the moon—no vegetation, no buildings, only charred rubble. Of the camp's inhabitants, only the prisoners and the remaining four guards are alive. Most of the population of Dresden is dead.

Billy travels in time to the Tralfamadore zoo, where he and Montana lie in bed together. Montana is six months pregnant. When she asks Billy to entertain her with a story, he responds with a description of the Allied bombing of Dresden on the night of February 13, 1945. He recounts how the prisoners are marched from the locker site to the hog sheds that had been their homes. Only the walls of the slaughterhouse are standing. Inside, the comprehension of the widespread devastation sets in—there is no water, no food, no shelter. Leaving the camp, the American prisoners and their guards climb and crawl through the smoking rubble of the city. American fighter planes, swooping down to see if anything is stirring, strafe them with their machine guns, but none of them are hit.

The guards and their prisoners continue struggling through the Dresden streets until nightfall, when they reach a suburb untouched by fire. At an inn run by a German couple and their two daughters, the four guards and the one hundred American POWs are fed. Later, the innkeeper offers rooms with beds to the Germans, but the Americans must sleep in the stable.

Commentary

The beginning of this chapter offers one of the novel's best character contrasts—that of Edgar Derby and Howard W. Campbell, Jr. Previously, Derby has seemed a rather pathetic figure, unable to act when faced with the contemporary problems of war that his high school students discussed. Now, prompted by the traitorous actions of Howard W. Campbell, Jr., he provides the most heroic action in the novel by standing up to Campbell. Verbally attacking the American Nazi, he defends the American prisoners' integrity.

Derby's active assault is in stark contrast to Campbell's demeanor. Clad in blue and white—colors that symbolize stasis, inaction, and death—Campbell baits the prisoners with promises of hearty meals in order to recruit them into his new organization, ironically called "The Free American Corps," even though there is nothing "free" about it. In this scene between the two men, Vonnegut juxtaposes the heroic resilience of the American prisoner with the deceptive, snakelike charm of the American traitor.

The conversation between Kilgore Trout and Maggie White at the Pilgrims' anniversary party provides Vonnegut the chance to comment on the authority bestowed on a writer by a gullible public. Similar to the theme of questioning authority highlighted in the comparison between Vonnegut and Kilgore Trout in Chapter Five, here Vonnegut suggests that writers create outlandish stories because the reading public wants them to. He criticizes readers who do not care enough to read books and are interested only in being superficially familiar with an author. Such a reader is Maggie White, who does not read books but adores authors. When Trout tells her that he could go to jail for fraud if he writes something that has not really happened, she believes him.

Vonnegut continues to add touches of irony to his text. The night of the Dresden bombing, as the Americans and four of their guards find refuge down in the meat locker, the other guards are at home "being killed with their families." Later, when Allied planes swoop down to strafe any survivors of the bombing, no one in Billy's entourage is hit. But near the river, the pilots manage to shoot some of their human targets. We are told that the machine-gunning of these unfortunates is an attempt to "hasten the end of the war," when, in fact, the American planes are firing on their fellow American soldiers. Sadly ironic scenes such as these sustain the tone of the novel.

The innkeeper's permitting the American prisoners to sleep in the stable furthers the biblical allusions in the novel. We recall the epigraph at the beginning of the novel: In the Christmas carol, the "little Lord Jesus" is born in a stable.

- **mince pie** a pie made from mincemeat, a mixture of finely chopped apples, raisins, spices, suet, and sometimes flavored with rum or brandy.

- **carbolic acid** a poisonous compound used in resins, plastics, and pharmaceuticals.

- **Crimea** a region and peninsula of southern Ukraine in eastern Europe, on the Black Sea.

- **Martha's Vineyard** an island off the southeast coast of Massachusetts known for its fabulously expensive living quarters and as an exclusive vacation resort.

- *Ivanhoe* an 1819 historical romance by Sir Walter Scott about the life of Sir Wilfred of Ivanhoe, a fictional Saxon knight.

- **calcimine** a white or tinted liquid used as a wash for walls and ceilings.

CHAPTER NINE

Summary

Following his tragic airplane accident, Billy lies in a Vermont hospital. Valencia sets out from Ilium, headed for Vermont to see him. In her frantic state, she has a car accident, yet she continues on to Vermont, minus the muffler to her car. As she turns off the car's ignition outside Billy's hospital, she falls unconscious, overcome by carbon monoxide. An hour later, Valencia is dead, her face an ashen blue.

Unconscious himself, Billy is unaware of Valencia's death. He shares a room with a retired brigadier general, Bertram Copeland Rumfoord, the official U.S. Air Force Historian and a professor at Harvard. Seventy years old and married to his twenty-three-year-old fifth wife, Lily, the professor is working on a book about the history of the U.S. Army Air Corps in World War II. Lily brings Rumfoord the books that he requests, including a copy of President Truman's announcement concerning the atomic bomb dropped on Hiroshima and a book about Dresden's destruction. The author of the Dresden book admits that the bombing was, indeed, a tragedy, but submits that those who approved the air raid were neither wicked nor cruel—it was simply one of those terrible things that sometimes happens in war.

After two brief time travels, the first to his office in Ilium in 1958, where he examines a patient's eyes, and the second to a day when he is sixteen years old and waiting to see a doctor for an infected thumb, Billy is visited in the Vermont hospital by his son, Robert. Robert is decorated with medals for being wounded in Vietnam. This is the young man who had such scholastic difficulty in his school years; now he is a model soldier. Billy closes his eyes and is unresponsive to Robert's presence.

While Billy lies in seeming unconsciousness, Rumfoord tells Lily about the bombing of Dresden. He is trying to condense twenty-seven volumes of air force history into one volume, but he has a problem concerning the Dresden bombing: It has been kept secret for so many years that American books make little mention of the event. Billy breaks his silence and tells Rumfoord that he was in Dresden when it was bombed, but Rumfoord does not take him seriously. He says that Billy is suffering from echolalia, a mental disease that makes people repeat things they hear.

Billy travels to 1945 Germany. It is two days after the end of the war in Europe, and he and five others are returning to the ruins of the slaughterhouse for souvenirs. Billy dozes in a horse-drawn wagon that they found, while his companions scour the camp. A middle-aged German couple passing by discovers that the horses are in a terrible state: Their mouths are bleeding, their hooves are broken, and they desperately need water. The couple scowl with reproach at Billy, who is still clownishly dressed in his azure toga and silver boots. They try to communicate with him using a number of languages. Discovering that he speaks English, they scold Billy for the condition of the horses. Suddenly aware of the horses' suffering, he bursts into tears. Up to now, he has not wept about any of the wartime atrocities that he has witnessed.

Billy travels in time back to the hospital in Vermont, and Rumfoord, who is beginning to become interested in what Billy says, satisfies himself that Billy has really been in Dresden. Billy tells the professor about the horses and the German couple, then describes how Russian soldiers arrived on motorcycles and arrested the Americans. Two days later, Billy Pilgrim was turned over to the Allies and shipped on a freighter home to America.

When Billy is released from the Vermont hospital, his daughter takes him home and puts him to bed, forbidding him to work or leave the house. But when a nurse hired to care for him is not looking, he sneaks out and drives to New York City, where he hopes to make an appearance on television and tell the world about the lessons he learned on Tralfamadore.

After checking into a hotel, he walks to Times Square and discovers a bookstore: In the back of the store, adults watch pornographic movies for twenty-five cents. Surrounded by hundreds of cheap books of pornography, he discovers four paperbacks by Kilgore Trout and buys one. He is unable to get a guest appearance on television, but he is booked for a radio talk show. A group of literary critics have gathered to discuss the purpose of writing novels; however, when Billy gets his turn, he speaks about flying saucers and Montana Wildhack. During the next commercial, he is gently expelled from the studio.

Billy returns to his hotel room, where he falls asleep and travels to Tralfamadore. When Montana asks him where he has been, he relates the events of his visit to New York City. He tells her that he bought one of Trout's books and saw part of a pornographic movie that she made. Montana's response shows that she has adopted Tralfamadorian philosophy: She feels free from guilt for having been a porn star.

Commentary

Vonnegut continues many of the same themes established in previous chapters, namely the color imagery and the biblical allusions. Overcome by carbon monoxide caused by the car accident, Valencia turns a "heavenly azure" as she dies. The azure of her death recalls the many references to blue and ivory, which denote stasis and death. The biblical allusion occurs when Billy dozes in the wagon and becomes aware of voices speaking in hushed tones. He imagines that the voices he hears are similar to the voices of those who removed Christ's body from the cross. Similar to the infant Jesus in the novel's epigraph, Billy is once again cast in the role of a Christ-figure. Aware of the horses' suffering, he bursts into tears. Later in life, he will weep uncontrollably in private.

The texts that Lily brings to Rumfoord are used by Vonnegut to demonstrate the official response to the brutality of World War II. Remembering that Rumfoord is the official U.S. Air Force Historian, and that he is attempting to condense a twenty-seven volume history of the air force into one volume, Vonnegut suggests that an "official response" to the bombing of Dresden, and, by association, the dropping of the atomic bomb on Japan, is ludicrous. The personal stories of the havoc caused by war, of which Billy's is just one example, are dismissed by those in charge. That the Dresden bombing was unfortunate is minimized by Rumfoord's assertion that it had to be done. Given the picture that Vonnegut presents of Dresden being a charming city without war factories or military installations, we conclude that Dresden did not need to be destroyed, that it offered no threat to the Allies, and that it was therefore mindlessly destroyed.

Throughout the novel, events separated by chronological time are often closely linked psychologically. One of the most poignant examples of this pairing concerns the elderly man in the waiting room with Billy when Billy is sixteen years old, and the hobo in previous chapters, who dies en route to the first camp that Billy and his fellow prisoners are taken. The elderly man in the waiting room apologizes profusely for his flatulence, telling Billy that he knew growing old would be bad, but he did not think that aging would be as bad as it really is. We are reminded of the hobo, who continually states that being taken prisoner and forced into a boxcar by Nazis is not as bad as it might seem. The hobo's repetitive assertion, that he has been in worse situations than the one he now finds himself in, ironically ceases when he dies on the ninth day of the journey. The general tone evoked by these two events contrasts Billy's clownish profile and makes the novel much more emotionally complex than we might at first believe it to be.

Billy's radio talk show appearance with literary critics affords Vonnegut the opportunity to lampoon those who would criticize his and other authors' novels. Previously, Vonnegut discussed the role of authors and the role of readers. Now he turns his attention to the critics and their puffed-up egos. Believing to know the reason why people read novels, one critic says that novels provide touches of color in rooms with all-white walls. Another submits that a novel's function is to teach wives of junior executives what to buy next and how to act in a French restaurant. Of course, Vonnegut is making fun of these assertions: Adding touches of color in rooms with all-white walls means nothing, and certainly novels do not help teach wives of junior executives how to act in French restaurants. Such comments suggest that literary critics perceive themselves as superior to other readers, a notion that Vonnegut is quick to ridicule.

- **Theodore Roosevelt** (1858–1919) the twenty-sixth president of the U.S. (1901–09); won the 1906 Nobel Peace Prize for his role in ending the Russo-Japanese War (1904–05).

- **Harry S Truman** (1884–1972) the thirty-third president of the U.S. (1945–53); authorized the use of the atomic bomb against Japan in 1945.

- **Pearl Harbor** the Hawaiian harbor where most of the U.S. naval fleet was when Japanese planes attacked without warning on December 7, 1941; afterward, the U.S. declared war against Japan.

- **V-1** a robot bomb deployed by the Germans in World War II.

- **V-2** a long-range, liquid-fuel rocket used by the Germans as a ballistic missile in World War II.

- **Buchenwald** a village in central Germany; site of a Nazi concentration camp during World War II.

- **Coventry** a city in central England that was heavily bombed by the Germans during World War II, laying waste to over 50,000 homes.

- **Purple Heart** a U.S. military decoration awarded to members of the armed forces wounded in action.

- **Silver Star** a U.S. military decoration awarded for gallantry, or courage.

- **Lucretia A. Mott** (1793–1880; middle initial is *C* for Coffin, not *A* as Vonnegut writes) American suffragist who advocated that women should have the same rights as men; Mott was instrumental in organizing the first convention for women's rights, held at Seneca Falls, New York, in 1848.

- **Appomattox** a town in south-central Virginia; on April 9, 1865, at the Appomattox Courthouse, General Robert E. Lee surrendered to General Ulysses S. Grant, ending the American Civil War.

- *Uncle Tom's Cabin* A novel by Harriet Beecher Stowe, published in book form in 1852, it dramatizes the plight of slaves and is often cited as one of the causes of the American Civil War.

- **Norman Mailer** American novelist born in 1923; best known for his World War II novel *The Naked and the Dead* (1948).

CHAPTER TEN

Summary

The final chapter begins in 1968, with the narrator providing a series of death reports: Robert Kennedy was shot two nights before, and Martin Luther King, Jr., was shot a month before. From Vietnam, the government provides daily body counts "created by military science." Billy reports that on Tralfamadore, there is little interest in Jesus Christ, but Tralfamadorians hold Charles Darwin in high regard. Darwin taught that "those who die are meant to die, and that corpses are improvements." From the Tralfamadorians, Billy learns that everyone lives forever, spending time reliving events over and over. The narrator is not overjoyed with Billy's epiphany, but, if it is true, then he is grateful that so many of his moments have been positive.

One of these positive experiences concerns his 1967 trip to Dresden with Bernard V. O'Hare. As they fly over East Germany, the narrator imagines dropping bombs on the villages and towns below. In a small notebook, O'Hare tries to find information on the population of Dresden, and he discovers statistics about a world population explosion and worldwide deaths due to malnutrition. The final sentence of the article in the notebook asserts that the world's population will be seven billion before the year 2000.

While the narrator and O'Hare fly to Dresden, Billy travels back to Dresden, two days after the city has been destroyed. Assigned to dig for bodies among the rubble, he is teamed with a Maori captured in Tobruk. Although many holes are dug in the rubble, most end when pavement is struck or large boulders are encountered. At last the diggers come to a structure of timbers that contains dozens of bodies. The opening is enlarged so that the corpses can be carried out.

Hundreds of corpse-yielding excavations are dug. The bodies begin to rot, and the stench becomes unbearable. The Maori gets sick and dies, vomiting in convulsions after he is ordered to work in one of the excavation caves. The Germans finally decide to stop bringing bodies to the surface; instead, they cremate them with flame throwers where they lie. While working in the excavations, Edgar Derby is discovered with a teapot in his possession. He is arrested for plundering, court-martialed, and executed.

Cremations stop when the German soldiers are called to fight the Russians. Billy and the other prisoners are locked up in a stable in the suburbs. One morning the prisoners awake to discover that the doors are unlocked: In Europe, World War II is over. The prisoners exit from their confinement and wander in the streets. The birds are talking, and one asks Billy Pilgrim, *"Poo-tee-weet?"*

Commentary

The final chapter concludes with a myriad of contrasts. The specter of murder in the beginning paragraphs is juxtaposed with a hint of renewed life in the final lines. The assassinations of Robert Kennedy and Martin Luther King, Jr., and the inhumanity of the body count from Vietnam are contrasted with Billy's wandering in the shady streets in springtime, with trees leafing out and birds singing. In addition, the assassinations remind us that Billy, like Kennedy and King, Jr., will also be killed by a bullet from a sniper's gun.

Chapter Ten also renders a final allusion to the theory of natural selection. With the death of the Maori, Vonnegut makes the same point he does with Edgar Derby: While both men are sound biological specimens, both fail to survive. Modern warfare does not reject the unsuitable and select the fittest for survival. Both Derby and the Maori, as well as those killed in the firestorm, are collectively eliminated without allowance for individual characteristics or distinctions, and those who survive do so without exhibiting any superior capabilities.

- **Robert Kennedy** (1925–68) American politician who served as U.S. Attorney General (1961–64) under his brother, President John F. Kennedy, and, after Kennedy's death, under President Lyndon B. Johnson; assassinated in Los Angeles by Sirhan Sirhan while campaigning for the presidency.

- **Martin Luther King, Jr.** (1929–68) American cleric and civil rights leader in the 1950s and 1960s; winner of the 1964 Nobel Peace Prize, four years before he was assassinated in Memphis, Tennessee.

- **Charles Darwin** (1809–82) British naturalist who developed a theory of evolution referred to today as Darwinism; Darwinism states that all species develop through natural selection based on the ability to survive and reproduce.

- **Adolphe Menjou** (1890–1963) twentieth-century film actor known for his character roles; among his films are *I Married a Woman* (1958) and *Step Lively* (1944).

- **Maori** a Polynesian people living in New Zealand, an island country in the South Pacific, southeast of Australia.

- **Tobruk** a city in northeast Libya on the southern shore of the Mediterranean Sea.

CRITICAL ESSAYS

PREDESTINATION AND FREE WILL
IN *SLAUGHTERHOUSE-FIVE*

The most significant theme in *Slaughterhouse-Five* concerns the dichotomy of predestination and free will. Over and over again, Vonnegut proclaims that there is no such thing as free will. Humankind is the slave of predestination, meaning that all human actions are prescribed before they occur. A person who chooses to do something is not really choosing at all—the choice is already made. This complicated issue can be confusing, but grasping the history of the arguments and Vonnegut's take on them will help us better understand and enjoy the novel.

The juxtaposition of predestination with the exercise of free will is as old as human thought itself. In the pagan world, before the rise of Western civilization and Christianity, the idea of predestination was accepted as truth. Pagan gods were supreme and decided the fates of humans, who had no effect on their own destiny. The belief in predestination was still commonly held throughout much of the medieval world. It was believed that an all-embracing plan was based in an aspect of God called Providence, and that the carrying out of Providence's decrees was delegated to a force called Destiny.

Sometime around 500 A.D., the Roman writer Boethius published a tract called *The Consolation of Philosophy*, a document that was instrumental in bringing about changes in philosophy in the Middle Ages. Boethius raised important questions: If things are predestined, humans do not have to worry about their own actions because they can blame their behavior on predestination. But if humans have a choice in whatever they do, then how can God truly have foreknowledge? Ultimately, Boethius acknowledged that God's foreknowledge and humans' free will are mutually exclusive: They have nothing to do with one another.

More than seven hundred years later, Thomas Aquinas corroborated Boethius' theory, but Aquinas' approach was somewhat different. Aquinas' explanation depended on the understanding that God exists and functions outside of time. God's being is measured not temporally, in terms of humans' notion of time, but by eternity, which overlaps the whole of time. The things that happen to humans at different times are, to God, "present time." Consequently, an event that is likely to happen is not future, but present. In short, God does not have foreknowledge as humans define it, but rather a knowledge of a never-changing present.

Vonnegut takes a clearly secular position concerning the dichotomy of predestination and free will. Although he includes many biblical allusions and offers a number of references to Christianity in *Slaughterhouse-Five*, he rejects Christianity as a truth unto itself, but he does ascribe to the principles of Christianity's philosophy. While most people choose sides in a conflict, Vonnegut's concept of our world affords him no earthly position of judgment. For example, he refuses to say if there is a right or a wrong side in waging modern warfare. Neither the Americans, nor the Japanese, nor even the Germans are more to blame for war's destruction.

Vonnegut assigns no fault, nor does he ask for punishment. Likewise, he never rewards his characters for their heroism, namely, because calling someone a hero means judging that person's actions as good, something Vonnegut will not do. The character who comes closest to being a hero is Edgar Derby, who stands up to the American Nazi Howard W. Campbell, Jr. But remember what absurdly happens to Derby shortly after the war ends: He is executed for stealing a teapot. Vonnegut never judges Derby, neither as a hero who deserves to be celebrated, nor as a thief who deserves to die. There are no heroes, there are no villains. Even Vonnegut's commentary on the assassinations of Robert Kennedy and Martin Luther King, Jr., two of America's most respected and beloved leaders, is the same as his comment on all death: *So it goes.* Vonnegut offers nothing further.

Vonnegut further emphasizes this notion of *So it goes* with the introduction of the Tralfamadorians' fourth-dimensional perception, which is similar to Aquinas' reconciliation of the dichotomy of predestination and free will. If one substitutes "Tralfamadorians" for "God" in Aquinas' thinking on the matter, the message rings the same. Things that occur at different times to humans are all in the present to Tralfamadorians, just as Aquinas argued that God perceives everything simultaneously, at once, and not in the future. In short, Tralfamadorians do not have foreknowledge as defined in human terms, but rather a knowledge of a never-changing present.

Billy Pilgrim, kidnapped by Tralfamadorians, is the only human—albeit Montana Wildhack, who is a special case—privy to Tralfamadorian philosophy. Aware that events in his life are predestined, Billy's time traveling remains different from that of his captors'. While Tralfamadorians see all events at once, Billy must be satisfied with his ability to travel from event to event without being able to experience two or more of these events at the same time—after all, the Tralfamadorians are amazed that Billy perceives time and events only in a three-dimensional view. Montana Wildhack's case is special if only because we never see her except in the Tralfamadore zoo. She is obviously aware of Billy's being unstuck in time, yet the narrator never mentions if she, too, is unstuck. Nevertheless, Billy and Montana are unique because both have traveled in time—for Montana, if only to the Tralfamadore zoo—and both are aware of their lives being predestined despite having only a three-dimensional vision of time.

THE ANTI-HERO AND BILLY PILGRIM

An anti-hero is defined as a fictional character occupying a pivotal role in a story and possessing traits contrasted with those of a traditional hero. The anti-hero, who usually appears absurdly fool-ish, is often the embodiment of ineptitude or bad luck. First used to describe such post-World War II characters as Yossarian in Joseph Heller's *Catch-22* (1961), earlier examples of the anti-hero can be dis-covered in novels as far back as Cervantes' *Don Quixote* (1605–15) or Laurence Sterne's *Tristram Shandy*, a century later. Whether found in seventeenth-century picaresque tales of chivalry or in the nose of a World War II bomber, the anti-hero manifests the same character-istics: He is weak, unskilled, uncultured, and lacking in both valor and dignity.

Billy Pilgrim is a classic anti-hero: He is a child of comical appearance who becomes a funny-looking youth. Throughout the novel, he is always referred to as "Billy," a diminutive form of "Wil-liam," which suggests that he remains child-like and never matures to adulthood. Even Ilium, the town he lives in his entire life, implies his anti-heroic stature. Ilium is the ancient name for Troy, a city of defiant, courageous warriors who lost the Trojan War; ironically, Billy is anything *but* a warrior.

During his stint in the army, he is lost behind enemy lines with no weapon, no coat, no helmet, and no boots, a wretched figure stumbling through the snow and the cold. With a heel missing from one of his shoes, he bobs up and down as he tries to keep up with his three fellow wanderers. A spindly scarecrow over six feet in height, with a torso that Vonnegut likens to a box of kitchen matches, Billy has no resemblance to the rugged, steel-eyed soldier traditionally depicted in films and novels as heroic, manly, and unquestioningly devoted to victory.

Throughout *Slaughterhouse-Five*, Billy is again and again the fool who is taken advantage of. Lacking the free will to make his own choices, he is foisted into roles that highlight his anti-heroic status. Shortly after Billy is captured in Luxembourg, a German war corre-spondent responsible for war propaganda takes photographs of him because he looks so outrageously inept. The pictures of his feet will be used as propaganda to show how poorly equipped the American army is. The photographer also wants pictures of Billy being taken prisoner, so the guards throw him in some bushes; with the guards wielding their weapons, a picture is snapped as he emerges. For the Germans, the picture makes a wonderful tool of propaganda be-cause Billy presents the American soldier as a pathetic oaf.

But the Germans are not alone in relegating Billy to a lowly status. Onboard a boxcar headed for the first POW camp, Billy finds a niche next to a ventilator. For two days the train does not move. Inside the boxcars, the prisoners excrete into their steel helmets, which are then passed to those standing at the ventilators, who dump them outside. Billy, lacking dignity and grace, is defined as a dumper. Arriving at the POW camp, he is once again cast as the fool. Instead of receiving a soldier's overcoat like those provided to all of his fellow prisoners, he is given a woman's coat with a fur collar. His farcical appearance especially draws the attention of the English colonel, who first asks Billy if the coat is a joke. Discovering that the Germans gave Billy the coat, the colonel exclaims that the coat is an insult, a deliberate attempt on the Germans' part to humiliate Billy. Later on, Billy acquires a pair of silver-painted boots and an azure-blue curtain that he dons like a toga. Combining these with the civilian coat, which he now wears like a muff, he becomes the definitive clown of World War II. When the POWs arrive in Dresden and climb down from the train, the German guards laugh uproariously at him. Even Dresden civilians smirk at his clownish garb. When a kitchen worker in the slaughterhouse sees his blue toga, silver boots, and furry muff, she asks him why he's dressed so ridiculously. He tells her that he is only trying to stay warm, yet his naïveté of how foolish he looks prompts her to compare him to other soldiers: She concludes that all of the heroic soldiers must be dead.

The casting of a clown-figure-as-hero is an old technique often used in literature to raise doubts about the reasoning of a protagonist such as a king or a prince, or, in the case of *Slaughterhouse-Five*, to question our assumptions not only about the right to wage war, but about the people who fight in war and the authorities who sanction the fighting. For instance, the fool in Shakespeare's *King Lear*, despite his verbal play, reveals a message taut with anxiety and perplexity, with distress and bitterness. Masquerading as song or witty poetry, the fool's message allows him to expose certain truths. But only the fool has that privilege: If others in the court dared to suggest such things, Lear would have them executed. The grave diggers in Shakespeare's *Hamlet* serve much the same purpose. These seemingly coarse and insignificant personalities do much more than provide comic relief in the midst of tragic action. Their conversation is fraught with profound musings on theological issues, and their dialogue contains Latin terms dealing with legal questions. But the incongruity of their lowly position contrasted with their profundity supplies the humor.

In *Slaughterhouse-Five*, the image of Billy as the clown, both pathetic and absurd, raises questions about the difference between illusion and reality. His anti-heroic status undermines our assumptions about soldiers who fight in war. Because we see Billy as an inept soldier, we therefore question the validity of the war in which he is fighting. In addition, remembering that Billy's son, Robert, is fighting in Vietnam, and that *Slaughterhouse-Five* was published in 1969, during the Vietnam War, the validity of that war is called into question as well. The authority figures responsible for the war, be they Bertram Copeland Rumfoord or Howard W. Campbell, Jr., are more likely to earn our condemnation when we see what kind of soldiers they send into action. The illusion of the heroic soldier icons (John Wayne, Frank Sinatra) depicted in films and in war propaganda is replaced in *Slaughterhouse-Five* by the reality of Billy Pilgrim.

THE VONNEGUT HUMOR

Vonnegut's humor is demonstrated primarily through the medium of black humor, a literary technique that makes us laugh so that we don't cry. Black humor is humor discovered in agony, despair, or horror. It can exist as an individualized hell or as a generally pessimistic view of the universe. In *Slaughterhouse-Five*, Vonnegut embellishes the scope of black humor by incorporating irony and by using vocabulary that creates a mock-serious tone, often leading to absurdity.

One example of Vonnegut's black humor concerns the British officers who welcome the American prisoners to the POW camp. These British officers, functioning in what would ordinarily be considered a demoralizing environment, manage to make the war experience seem less horrific than it really is. They treat the American POWs to a musical version of *Cinderella* during the first night in camp, an entertaining fare one would not typically expect in a German POW camp. With their incredible morale and elevated *esprit*, the British officers delight even the Germans who hold them captive. However, juxtaposed to this fantastical way of life is the fact that the Englishmen readily use objects of inhumanity without remorse. For example, their candles and soap, made from human fat rendered from Nazi war victims, are accepted without question. *Slaughterhouse-Five* is replete with such horrible compromise, yet the severity of these events is masked by Vonnegut's black humor.

On an individual level, the best examples of the novel's ironic black humor concern the hobo and Edgar Derby. The forty-year-old hobo, captured along with the American soldiers, continually assures his comrades that things "ain't so bad." He has been in box-cars before, he announces, but after nine days of confinement, he dies. Such situational irony is also evident in Derby's plight. He sur-vives the bombing of Dresden, but he does not survive what fol-lows. Having stolen a teapot, a minuscule item indeed, he is executed for the offense. For Vonnegut, the personal irony of the hobo's and Derby's situations magnifies the injustices of war, which often lead to the demise of individuals and their untimely deaths in absurd circumstances.

One additional technique that Vonnegut employs to set the tone of the novel's black humor is his use of words or phrases as a form of mock seriousness that gives way to the absurd. On the night of the Dresden bombing, Billy and his fellow POWs, as well as some of the guard detail, are underground in a meat locker that is used as a bomb shelter. Vonnegut's use of the term "meat locker" emphasizes that the prisoners are viewed not as humans by their captors, but as animals; after all, they are held in a slaughterhouse for animals. Just as animals were previously killed in the Dresden slaughterhouse, so too, in theory, will many prisoners and civilians be killed—only the killers will not be Germans, but rather the American prisoners' fellow Allied soldiers. Other German guards, Vonnegut tells us, have "gone to the comforts of their own homes in Dresden. They were all being killed with their families." This tone of irony contrasts the human condition of life and family with the despair of death.

Another example of mock seriousness dissolving into absurdity is demonstrated in the dialogue of Wild Bob, the American infantry colonel who loses his entire regiment in battle. Waiting to be loaded into the boxcars destined for the POW camp, Wild Bob assures his men that there are dead Germans lying all over the battlefield who despair to God that they ever encountered the 405th Infantry Regiment, the regiment under Wild Bob's command. The serious-ness of the situation quickly descends to absurdity as we realize that Wild Bob, critically injured and about to die, is losing his mind. The men to whom he speaks are not even part of his former regiment, yet Wild Bob hallucinates that they are. Even more pathetically absurd is his notion that the Germans died wishing they had never heard of his regiment: Wild Bob's soldiers, *not* the Germans, died on that battlefield.

THE PRESENCE OF THE NARRATOR
IN *SLAUGHTERHOUSE-FIVE*

In *Slaughterhouse-Five*, Vonnegut takes an omniscient point of view, electing to be both inside and above the action of the text. Such a position allows him to go beyond the limits of the characters' perceptions in order to let us know what is happening both on Earth and on Tralfamadore at any given time. Vonnegut's telling us things that the characters cannot know gives us a broader perspective of time and space in the novel.

In addition to being the narrator, Vonnegut is present within the text as the narrative's central character in the first and last chapters. He appears in the text on three occasions to remind us that, although he is now above the novel's actions and is reflecting on the past events, he was once part of the action.

Along with Vonnegut's being an omniscient narrator, he demands that we participate in the narrative. He connects events that are not chronologically linear, but that exist harmoniously in psychological time. We must learn to infer transitions and to make equations between these images: In so doing, we relive—like the Tralfamadorians and Billy Pilgrim—past moments with the added knowledge of the future of those moments.

A first-time reader of *Slaughterhouse-Five* is likely to pass over Vonnegut's short bursts of imagery without any particular notice. Many of these images, recalled when something similar happens at a later time or in another place, connect and reconnect the novel's themes. For example, the appearance of Vonnegut's first dog not only recalls his second dog, it invokes the events of the time when the second dog appears. In turn, both dogs recall not just the presence of the German shepherd dog in Luxembourg, but the events that take place at that time. And likewise, the image of the golden cavalry boots worn by the old German corporal not only foreshadows the image of Billy's silver boots, but also events from both perspectives in time. These images are important because they help link together different scenes that occur at different times. Although individual events in *Slaughterhouse-Five* seem fragmented at first, Vonnegut's imagery makes the novel a cohesive whole.

THE SONG OF ROLAND AND SLAUGHTERHOUSE-FIVE

In the many wars fought throughout history, the proclamation "God is on our side!" has been used as propaganda to justify the validity of waging battle. Warring parties often use God's blessing to rationalize the killing of human beings. In *Slaughterhouse-Five*, Vonnegut examines the nature of this self-righteous proclamation through the creation of the character Roland Weary. Until his death in Chapter Four, Weary serves as a contrast to the medieval French knight Roland, a character immortalized in the French ballad *La Chanson de Roland (The Song of Roland)*, who commanded the withdrawal of French troops during an eighth-century battle fought by Roland's uncle, Charlemagne. Vonnegut parodies Weary's actions in World War II to the actions of the French knight to show that wars are still fought by armies proclaiming God's support when, in fact, they are never divinely justified. To better understand the relationship between the French knight Roland and Vonnegut's Roland Weary, we should review the French knight's tale; only then can we grasp Vonnegut's intentions in *Slaughterhouse-Five*.

During the Middle Ages, French troubadours, or minstrels, sang of the deeds of Charlemagne and his followers in a number of ballads, including *La Chanson de Roland*, which relates an incident during the withdrawal of Charlemagne's armies from Spain. In the *Chanson*, Charlemagne wages a campaign of some thirty years throughout Europe and the Middle East to defend onslaughts by heathen Saxons and other non-Christians. In one of these campaigns, Charlemagne carries out an operation against a group of Spaniards, the Saracen Muhammadans. After receiving the surrender of all of their towns and fortresses, he prepares to return to France. To carry out a successful withdrawal, he places his nephew, Roland, in command of the rear guard.

In a dense forest on top of a mountain, the Saracen Muhammadans ambush Roland's troops. Seeing that he is overpowered by the attackers, Roland is urged to sound a horn that will signal trouble and bring the main body of Charlemagne's army to the rescue. Out of arrogance and overconfidence, however, he refuses to blow the horn: He savors the opportunity to defeat the entire Saracen army with his own small body of soldiers. Surprisingly, the French manage to hold their own in four separate skirmishes, but the fifth battle is a disaster, and Roland now chooses to sound the horn. For the sake of honor, his close comrade, Oliver, feels it would be shameful to summon Charlemagne to see the tragedy, for already it is too late for him to help them. Roland acknowledges that the battle is lost and that his soldiers will be killed, but he insists on summoning Charlemagne. Wounded and bleeding profusely, he fights on. He climbs a hill and, preparing to die, prays to God, asking forgiveness for his sins. Crying out to God, he dies. *The Song of Roland* ends with Roland's soul being carried up to heaven by Saint Michael, the Archangel Gabriel, and a spirit with golden wings.

Drawing on this tale, Vonnegut develops a parallel between Private Roland Weary and the French knight. In *Slaughterhouse-Five*, Weary carries a whistle that he plans to keep hidden until he gets promoted. His whistle corresponds to the horn that Roland carries, and which he plans to use only if he needs his uncle's help. Weary's imagination leads him to fantasize that he and the two scouts with whom he wanders in the forest are as inseparable as the Three Musketeers, even though the scouts eventually leave Weary and Billy to wander in the woods alone. In the French ballad, Roland and his companion, Oliver, are portrayed as inseparable comrades, although they argue over whether or not to blow the horn. In *Slaughterhouse-Five*, the German soldiers have no trouble following the Americans, including Billy, because they leave tracks in the snow. On the Spanish border, the Saracen Muhammadans have no trouble following Roland, whose withdrawal route they know beforehand because a traitor has divulged the plans.

In Chapter Three, Billy, a pacifist, rather than Weary, a man who delights in physical cruelty, looks at a young German soldier and likens the youth to a blond angel, an important image that recalls the spirit with golden wings who carries the French knight Roland's soul up to heaven. By having Billy—and not Weary—see what he thinks is an angel, Vonnegut turns the similarities between *The Song of Roland* and *Slaughterhouse-Five* upside down. Because the French knight's soul is lifted to heaven by angels, we would expect the same for Weary, who is similar to his namesake in many of the actions he performs. However, Vonnegut suggests that God is not on anyone's side in war. After all, the French knight and Weary are both soldiers, yet Weary sees no angels when he dies. Ironically, it is Billy, the character most *un*like a soldier, who sees the angel-like youth. Using the analogy of *The Song of Roland*, Vonnegut shows that the notion of God as an ally, or a partner, in war is not true. Instead, such a self-righteous notion is simply a tool of propaganda, used to validate one warring party over another.

SLAUGHTERHOUSE-FIVE ON FILM

Only one movie has been produced from Vonnegut's novel: the 1972 film directed by George Roy Hill (who also directed the 1969 *Butch Cassidy and the Sundance Kid*), and starring Michael Sacks as Billy, Valerie Perrine as Montana, Sharon Gans as Valencia, Ron Leibman as Lazzaro, and Eugene Roche as Derby. While the novel's readers will undoubtedly follow the frequent switching between scenes in the movie better than viewers who have not read the book, the film's "plot" is accessible to newcomers of the cinematic version of *Slaughterhouse-Five*.

Certain elements in the film will stand out to the person who has both read the novel and viewed the movie. These include the lack of the narrator/Kurt Vonnegut figure as a framing device; Hill's creating visual scenes and settings by using music and the color white; and the visually successful seguing devices (not possible in a book) that facilitate the juxtaposition of scenes. In all, the movie is a fair and arresting representation of Vonnegut's novel about the bombing of Dresden.

What is most noticeable to the film viewer who has read the book is the disappearance of the first and last chapters of the book. There is no mention of Bernard V. O'Hare or his wife, Mary, nor does Hill film Vonnegut and O'Hare's traveling to Dresden after the war to revisit the site of the horrible destruction. Instead, the movie begins with Billy's daughter, Barbara, and her husband banging on Billy's front door, worried that something might be wrong. Billy is oblivious to them and is at his typewriter, composing a letter that recounts his being kidnapped by Tralfamadorians. The constant switching between scenes that occurs in the movie is explained by a close-up shot of what Billy is typing: "I have come unstuck in time."

Ironically, the movie's most recognizable framing device is Montana Wildhack, who does not appear in the first half of the novel. Ignoring Barbara's pounding on his door, Billy looks up from typing and envisions Montana. Although this reference to Montana so early in the film lasts only briefly, it is one of the first "trips" Billy takes. This scene contrasts with the last scene in the movie, when Montana is breast-feeding her and Billy's baby boy. The scene just prior to this one involves Billy getting stuck under a grandfather clock that Paul Lazzaro looted from a shop after the war but abandoned when Russian soldiers approached him. If we understand Billy's getting caught under the clock as his becoming *stuck* in time, this idea suggests that the final scene with Montana is one from which Billy will not travel; or, his future life with Montana will be more enjoyable than any life-on-earth experience that he has previously had. Certainly, the fireworks that end the movie suggest a festive celebration of Billy, Montana, and their baby together.

Two other differences are notable in the film: the importance of Paul Lazzaro and the absence of Kilgore Trout. Whereas in the book Roland Weary and Billy are captured by the German soldiers and their dog, in the film version it is Lazzaro who is captured with Billy. Weary does not appear until later, when Billy continually walks on his feet while they are marching to the Russian prison camp, an offense for which Lazzaro will eventually kill Billy. In the film, Lazzaro is not depicted as the frail man that he is in the novel. In the novel, he is described as "tiny" and is referred to by the English soldiers as a chicken because of his small, spindly body. However, from the start of the movie, Lazzaro is the camp bully, who goes so far as to pick fights with German soldiers. He threatens not only Billy and Edgar Derby, but every person with whom he comes in contact. Ironically, the one redeeming value granted him is when he threatens Howard W. Campbell, Jr., who has come to the camp to enlist American POWs to fight for the Germans. When Campbell asks for recruits, Lazzaro gets out of his seat and walks toward Campbell. Bomb sirens sound, and we are left with the impression that Lazzaro is going to join Campbell. However, once the prisoners and their guards—including Campbell—are assembled in the slaughterhouse basement, Lazzaro informs a suspecting Derby that he was going to hit Campbell, not join him. The revelation hardly endears Lazzaro to Derby—or to us.

The absence of Kilgore Trout is understandable. In Vonnegut's book, the interplay between Trout and Billy highlights Vonnegut's commentary on the nature of writing. Trout is the device that Vonnegut uses to point out how unsuspecting and gullible readers can be, and how conceited writers and critics can become. Obviously, the film version of *Slaughterhouse-Five* makes Trout's role obsolete.

Whereas authors depend on readers to make a scene come alive when reading descriptions that the author provides, a film director has a much easier challenge. Hill integrates music and the color white to achieve depth to the scenes. Often, these two aspects are used in tandem. This coupling happens in the first war scene in the movie. Billy is lost behind enemy lines and appears to be wandering aimlessly. His isolation is heightened by the scene's background music, a classical piece by Johann Sebastian Bach that sounds very plodding, but is filled with many piano trills. By juxtaposing this baroque music with Billy's obviously hopeless state, Hill emphasizes the despair of Billy's situation. We would expect heavy, loud music in a movie about war, but Hill supplies the opposite. The white snow on the ground and the vast whiteness of the sky isolates Billy—there are no objects that locate him in a familiar surrounding. He seems thrown onto a canvas of white, a color that symbolizes purity—which Billy is—but it also symbolizes isolation.

Contrasted to the effect that Hill creates in this scene is the later one in which Billy and his fellow prisoners arrive in Dresden and then march through the city. Again, Hill uses classical music, this time Bach's Fourth Brandenburg Concerto. The music is jubilant and uplifting, a joyous sound that the viewer associates with celebration and festivity. The music selection undercuts the solemnity of the situation and emphasizes the naiveté of the marching soldiers, as do the children who skip around the soldiers and tug at their hands. Against the white and hazy sky of Dresden—used by Hill to create a feeling of isolation of the city from the world—are close-up shots of carved statues that stand atop beautifully maintained buildings. The statues appear to be staring down at the marching soldiers; we are unsure whether the statues are condemning the soldiers, pitying their circumstances, or merely bearing witness. In all, the effect produced by Hill is masterful.

One reason why the film version of the movie is easier to follow than we might expect is Hill's use of "triggers," or devices that link scenes together, which Vonnegut obscured in the novel. One of the more obvious triggers in the film involves the election of Edgar

Derby as leader of the American prisoners and the election of Billy as president of Ilium's Lions Club. In the scene when Derby is chosen as the leader, Billy is the lone prisoner who claps as Derby approaches a stage from which to address his fellow Americans. The scene then shifts abruptly to Billy's walking to a dais to speak and his fellow Lions Club members loudly applaud. Cutting back to the war scene, Derby begins addressing the prisoners, but the scene switches suddenly to Billy's speech: He begins his speech the exact same way that Derby does his. Although both men deliver their speeches at different times in history, Hill parallels the scenes by having Billy mimic the beginning of Derby's address as his own. The clapping and the speeches are triggers that link these two scenes together so that we can better grasp and appreciate Vonnegut's black humor and irony.

One other notable instance of triggers involves the American soldiers' emerging from the bomb shelter and Billy's retiring upstairs at his home after returning from the hospital. In each case, the trigger that links the scenes is a shot of legs ascending stairs. In the war scene, the prisoners climb the flight of stairs to discover the horror of a burning Dresden. We expect this desolation to carry over into Billy's life—he has just returned home from the plane crash and his wife is dead. However, what ensues after Billy takes a nap in his bedroom is the Tralfamadorians' taking him to their planet. Given the earlier discussion of Billy's apparently happy existence on Tralfamadore, the desolation of the bombed Dresden does not carry over into Billy's later life.

As one critic notes, the film version of *Slaughterhouse-Five* is more easily understood the more times it is viewed. And certainly, reading the novel before watching the movie helps. But all in all, Hill's repeating visual themes, such as the color white and the triggers that link scenes together, make the film accessible to a first-time viewer.

REVIEW QUESTIONS AND ESSAY TOPICS

(1). Discuss the paradox of free will and predestination. In *Slaughterhouse-Five*, is anyone able to exercise free will, or are all things predetermined? How would characters such as Bertram Copeland Rumfoord or Kilgore Trout answer these questions? Defend your answer. What about them would make them feel that way?

(2). Discuss the meaning of Harrison Starr's proclamation that it is futile to write an antiwar novel. What does he mean when he asks the narrator, "Why don't you write an anti-*glacier* book, instead?"

(3). The colors of the banners flying on the POW train and the colors of the tent set up for Billy's daughter's wedding are orange and black. What is the significance of these colors in the novel?

(4). What is the significance of the colors blue and ivory, used throughout *Slaughterhouse-Five*? Other than orange, black, blue, and ivory, are there any other colors that carry symbolic weight in the novel? What are these colors' significance?

(5). How does Vonnegut interpret Gerhard Müller's comment about their meeting in the future "if the accident will"? Why does Müller use the word "accident" when speaking of the future?

(6). Why does Mary O'Hare berate Kurt Vonnegut, assuming that he is going to write a war novel whose heroes could be portrayed in a movie starring John Wayne or Frank Sinatra? What type of characters do these two actors usually portray on film? What is Mary O'Hare worried about?

(7). In civilian life, Edgar Derby teaches a course called "Contemporary Problems in Western Civilization." In view of Derby's circumstances, why is the title of the course ironic?

(8). How does Vonnegut express the Maori's death in terms of Darwinian theory?

(9). How does the epigraph relate to Billy Pilgrim? Does the Epigraph relate to any other character in the novel? If so, how? If not, why not?

(10). How does the cyclic poem about Yon Yonson relate to the narrative and structural form that Vonnegut uses in his composition of *Slaughterhouse-Five*?

VONNEGUT'S PUBLISHED WORKS

Fiction

Player Piano (1952)
The Sirens of Titan (1959)
Mother Night (1961)
Cat's Cradle (1963)
God Bless You, Mr. Rosewater (1965)
Slaughterhouse-Five (1969)
Breakfast of Champions, or Goodbye, Blue Monday (1973)
Slapstick (1976)
Jailbird (1979)
Deadeye Dick (1982)
Galapagos (1985)
Bluebeard (1987)
Hocus Pocus (1990)

Drama

Happy Birthday, Wanda June (1970)
Between Time and Timbuktu, or Prometheus-5 (1972)

Collections of Short Stories

Canary in a Cathouse (1961)
Welcome to the Monkey House (1970)

Essays

Wampeters, Foma & Granfalloons (1965)
Palm Sunday (1981)
Fates Worse Than Death (1991)

SELECTED BIBLIOGRAPHY

ALLEN, WILLIAM RODNEY. *Conversations with Kurt Vonnegut.* Jackson: University Press of Mississippi, 1988.

_____. *Understanding Kurt Vonnegut.* Columbia: University of South Carolina Press, 1991.

BROER, LAWRENCE R. *Sanity Plea: Schizophrenia in the Novels of Kurt Vonnegut.* Tuscaloosa: University of Alabama Press, 1994.

CRICHTON, J. MICHAEL. "Sci-Fi and Vonnegut." *New Republic* 2 April 1969: 33–35.

FREESE, PETER. "Kurt Vonnegut's *Slaughterhouse-Five*; Or, How to Storify an Atrocity." *Historiographic Metafiction in Modern American and Canadian Literature.* Eds. Bernd Engler and Kurt Muller. Paderborn: Ferdinand Schoningh Publishers, 1994.

HICKS, GRANVILLE. "Literary Horizons." *Saturday Review* 29 March 1969: 25.

IRVING, DAVID. *The Destruction of Dresden.* New York: William Kimber and Co. Ltd., 1963.

KLINKOWITZ, JEROME. *Slaughterhouse-Five: Reforming the Novel and the World.* Boston: Twayne Publishers, 1990.

_____. "*Slaughterhouse-Five*: Fiction into Film." *Take Two: Adapting the Contemporary American Novel to Film.* Ed. Barbara Tepa Lupack. Bowling Green, Ohio: Popular Publishers, 1994.

KLINKOWITZ, JEROME, and DONALD L. LAWLER. *Vonnegut in America: An Introduction to the Life and Work of Kurt Vonnegut.* New York: Delacorte Press, 1977.

KLINKOWITZ, JEROME, and JOHN SOMER, eds. *The Vonnegut Statement.* New York: Dell Publishing Company, 1973.

LEEDS, MARC. *The Vonnegut Encyclopedia: An Authorized Compendium*. Westport, Connecticut: Greenwood, 1995.

LUNDQUIST, JAMES. *Kurt Vonnegut*. New York: Frederick Ungar Publishing Company, 1977.

MERRILL, ROBERT, ed. *Critical Essays on Kurt Vonnegut*. Boston: G. K. Hall and Company, 1990.

MORSE, DONALD E. " 'Why Not You?': Kurt Vonnegut's Debt to the Book of Job." *Eger Journal of American Studies* 1 (1993): 75–88.

NOGUCHI, KENJI. "Vonnegut's Desperado Humor in *Slaughterhouse-Five*." *Studies in English Language and Literature* 45 (February 1995): 1–15.

REED, PETER J. *Writers for the Seventies: Kurt Vonnegut, Jr.* New York: Warner Books, Inc., 1972.

REED, PETER J., and PAUL BAEPLER. "A Selected Bibliography, 1985–1992." *Bulletin of Bibliography* 50.2 (June 1993): 123–28.

ROETHKE, THEODORE. "The Waking." *The Collected Poems of Theodore Roethke*. Garden City, New York: Anchor Books, 1975.

SCHATT, STANLEY. *Kurt Vonnegut, Jr.* Boston: Twayne Publishers, 1976.

SCHOLES, ROBERT. *The Fabulators*. New York: Oxford University Press, 1967.

_____. "Like Lot's Wife, He Looked Back—at the Destruction of Dresden and 135,000 Dead." *New York Times Book Review* 6 April 1969: 1–23.

The Song of Roland. Trans. Frederick Bliss Luquiens. New York: Collier Books, Inc., 1967.